University Adult Education in London

A CENTURY OF ACHIEVEMENT

John Burrows

THE WORKING MEN'S COLLEGE

AUSPICIUM MELIORIS

ÆVI. MDCCCLIV.

Purchased

1913

UNIVERSITY OF LONDON
SENATE HOUSE

Distributed by
National Institute of Adult Education
De Montfort House, Leicester

Contents

Foreword

Participation of the universities in adult education is still something exceptional in the world today. Only in the English-speaking countries do they play an important rôle in this field. Elsewhere universities have kept aloof, perhaps because they wished to maintain a certain academic exclusiveness, keeping their distance by the use of a special kind of language not accessible to ordinary men, but also because they wanted to keep out of the market place for fear that this would mean lowering their standards or damage their prestige.

As so often in England, it was probably a mixture of idealism and an uneasy conscience at the lack of equal opportunities which led to the movement that wanted to extend the opportunities for some share in university education to a wider public. London, as John Burrows shows in this lucid and engaging study, was one of the first universities in this field.

University extension has not only served the community by its contribution to intellectual advance and social progress, it has also been of benefit to the universities themselves – by extending their influence and indeed their knowledge of the society that sustains them. More, it has promoted the multiplication of the universities themselves since many of them owe their foundation to the extension movement.

As R. H. Tawney argued in his book on *Equality* 'social well-being does not only depend on intelligent leadership; it also depends on cohesion and solidarity. It implies the existence, not merely of opportunities to ascend, but of a high level of general culture, and a strong sense of common interests, and the diffusion throughout society of a conviction that civilisation is not the business of an elite alone, but a common enterprise which is the concern of all.'

It would be hard to find a more succinct account of the central purposes of adult education than these two sentences. And it is notable that even in a book inspired by a deep and passionate belief in equality Tawney did not demand that the elite should be abolished. He wanted to see the opportunities enjoyed by the elite opened up and expanded, and adult education was to be the instrument. Like Matthew Arnold he must have been convinced that 'the men of culture are the true apostles of equality'. And that culture was to be both general and diffused. By appealing to the universities the movement for workers' education which Tawney helped to inspire showed that it rejected the notion of a class culture: there was one culture, not two, and the workers were claiming their rightful share in it. Their demands, voiced by the WEA after the turn of the century, gave an essential new impetus to the movement which extended university education.

Naturally, adult education could not be and has not been the only agency of cultural advance. Changes in political attitudes, in the social structure and the educational system were essential conditions, but adult education was indispensable in helping to bring about these changes. In fact it has had an impact far greater than the number of people engaged in it would seem to imply because many of them were also prominently active in other fields.

The universities have been the backbone of the adult education movement throughout its modern history, first by the development of extension courses and later by the establishment of specialist departments for extra-mural studies which also gave support to the WEA. It was a development of which the universities can rightly be proud. They have helped, to quote Tawney once more, to create 'a common affection for the qualities which belong, not to any class or profession of men, but to man himself'.

One of the most striking features of extra-mural studies over the last hundred years has been the adaptability to the changing needs and demands of adult students. Forms have perhaps changed less than content. The well-known English ability to put new wine into old bottles has once again been convincingly demonstrated here and London, in common with other universities, provides a comprehensive range of higher education opportunities beyond the walls.

The composition of extra-mural classes was bound to change as society changed. Certainly there are not enough industrial workers in these classes but this has been a perennial weakness and is something which was true almost from the very start. It equally affects the Open University which was established partly to break out of this limitation and which has, through radio and television, direct access to practically every home in the country.

Well before the end of the last century, Lady Bracknell pointed out that Gwendolen had left her unhappy father 'under the impression that she is attending a more than usually lengthy lecture by the University Extension Scheme on the influence of a permanent income on Thought'. There was not even an indication by Oscar Wilde that Gwendolen wanted to go in for social research or join a workers' organisation.

Some even-handed justice may be at work in this vital rôle of the middle class in adult education. After all it is only fair that members of the class whose representatives—from Marx to Mao and Marcuse—have done so much to tear society apart, should try to put it together again. For as we daily learn afresh, without some common ground, some agreed purpose, some social contract, democracy cannot function and liberty may be lost.

The adult class is not merely an instrument of learning; it is a place where people from quite different backgrounds can together practice some of the virtues of democracy. In some way these small groups are replicas of society where the art of self-government can be practised. Ideally their members develop critical awareness, independence of judgment and skills of self-expression, all of which are essential in a free society.

One effect of the rising standard of general education—to which radio and television have made a prodigious contribution—has been to multiply the demand for adult education and many of the adult students who are now considered to be middle-class do in fact come from working-class backgrounds. The new social climate has stimulated their desire to study. And you can only begin to teach when there is the wish to learn.

As John Burrows shows, London is unique in its extra-mural studies not only for the size and variety of its annual programme but also for its wide range of diplomas and certificates to be obtained in part-time study by adult students. As elsewhere, the barriers formerly dividing liberal and vocational education have been broken down and a great deal of the new development of recent years has been in areas where general and vocational interests meet.

Specialist tutors have been appointed whose main purpose it is to conduct courses of a high standard for industrial workers, particularly shop-stewards and trades union secretaries. New approaches have also been made by the appointment of a staff lecturer in community studies based in an area where, with the help of the staff of an ILEA Adult Education Institute, he can establish a network of contacts with local working-class people and provide a programme of activities which meet their educational needs.

A great deal of very successful work is also being done in special courses for people engaged in social work, scientific activities, the arts, transport and communications. Others cater for magistrates, police officers and, more recently, officers of the three services. Members of these courses are encouraged to examine against an academic background the work they are engaged in and to make contact with others who have different functions in the same or neighbouring fields. A long-established section in the department is responsible for a variety of vocational diplomas and certificates ranging from nursing to field biology. Over 5,000 adult students are now registered in this section alone. Altogether over 20,000 students take part in London's extra-mural courses every year.

Here then is a convincing demonstration that the University looks upon education throughout life as an active obligation and not just an ideal for the future. That future was to be brought nearer by the detailed recommendations of the Russell Committee whose report was published in 1973. At that time the Russell Committee was widely criticised because its demands, although thoroughly workmanlike, were not considered to be sufficiently dramatic. How absurd much of this criticism now seems, only three lean years later, when we should be thoroughly delighted to receive half that loaf! That would also help us to bridge the fateful gap between the school-leaving age and the revival of educational interest which occurs in adult life, a gap which for many industrial workers in particular makes it so difficult to recover the skills indispensable for study.

The funds devoted to the education of adults – that is, to those who pay the taxes – have remained negligible compared with those made available in other fields of education. Yet, as the Russell Committee said, there exists within our community an enormous reservoir of human and material resources. A relatively modest investment in adult education could release those resources for the benefit of individuals and the good of society. R. D. Roberts, the first secretary of the University's Extension Department, wanted to make possible 'an education that enriches life, that stirs the imagination, that clears the mind of narrowness and prejudice, that trains the critical faculty to form some judgments.' And as he emphasised, it is a charge upon the universities 'to bring within the reach of the whole of the adult population such facilities as would give all who chose to make use of them the chance of becoming life-long students'.

Impressive arguments have recently been put forward in favour of combining in each university under a single board traditional adult education and all other university part-time education. The demand has been prompted by the growth of part-time and post-experience studies which need similar services, and by the recognition that the adult education departments have on their staff, in the words of Sir Derman Christopherson, the vice-chancellor of Durham University 'the most successful practitioners of the art of teaching that the university has'. It is a tempting prospect for those who are attracted by the economies of scale as well as for empire builders, but there is an obvious risk that in such a vast department those students who are driven by a desire for deeper knowledge rather than promotion might find themselves near the bottom of the scale of priorities, since their courses are least likely to attract the generous financial support which industry and commerce are prepared to give to postgraduate and post-experience courses leading to an obvious gain in professional competence. The risks of such a development have already been demonstrated by the huge extension divisions of some American universities, where liberal studies have either been swamped by professional courses or have never got off the ground.

Extra-mural departments ought to concentrate on those fields of study – mainly in the humanities, of which science forms part – where they can make an academic contribution, as distinct from becoming some kind of service department, laying pipes through which others pump their knowledge. And they would betray their true function if they ceased to be outward looking and came to consider it their main task to arrange postgraduate refresher courses for those who have already enjoyed the benefits of a university education.

There can be no doubt that university adult education still has before it a tremendous task: to help more and more people find their own and their country's place in the world, and to increase the number of those who make their contribution to the energies which sustain and renew our civilisation.

WERNER BURMEISTER

Preface

Unlike other centennial accounts of various aspects of the history of the University of London what follows is more in the nature of a sketch rather than a definitive work.

Several colleagues in the Department of Extra-Mural Studies have given much help and guidance – Werner Burmeister, now retired from the directorship has been a constant source of encouragement and advice; the two deputy directors, Cyril Thomas and T. F. Evans have likewise been helpful in recalling events of post-war development; Ronald Knowles with his unrivalled knowledge of the work spanning some four decades produced original material especially on vocational awards and the summer school in English – his foresight in collating minutes and agenda during the war and immediate post-war period has forestalled what would have been a considerable lacuna in the records, already sadly depleted; Fred Brook, formerly deputy director, has contributed some interesting material on the early days of the tutorial class movement, which was supplemented by Jack Pavey from his unique collection of literature.

The basic tedious task of transmuting an inelegantly handwritten manuscript into a neat piece of typescript for the printer was achieved by several secretaries in the department, including Miss Ann Appleby, Miss Dorothy Clingo, Mrs Margaret Robertson and Miss Anne Spurway. Finally the staff of the Goldsmiths' Library have responded to frequent requests for literature, especially from the university archives, whilst the Printing Section have demonstrated their skill on the productive side. To these colleagues and others not mentioned by name, I owe a great debt of gratitude.

Adult education is not normally an area of contention, except in times of financial stringency when it usually has to bear the brunt of economies, more likely to be petty rather than punitive. In London, however, the two sides of the work, university extension and tutorial classes have sometimes produced a tension, never destructive, but frequently creative. Any comments on this and other developments are entirely the responsibility of the author, as are his opinions and interpretations of earlier phases of the history.

JOHN BURROWS

The Work of the London Society

There is no single answer to the question: 'why were university extension lectures held for the first time in London during autumn 1876?' One explanation would be that Cambridge had first organised local lectures (as they were called) in 1873 largely due to the drive and imagination of James Stuart[1] at a time when the ancient university was bestirring itself to meet the needs of a rapidly changing society. Circumstances were different in London where the University (founded in 1836) was restricted to the limited, though increasingly important, tasks of conducting examinations and awarding degrees.

Other organisations providing adult classes for Londoners included Birkbeck Institution (founded in 1823 as the London Mechanics Institution, and since 1920, Birkbeck College, a school of the University) and the Working Men's College. Of the two university establishments, University College and King's College, the latter, after an abortive start in 1849, had established an evening department in 1855, colourfully described by Dickens in *Household Works*, 1858, as the 'college by gaslight in the Strand'.

Its courses in liberal and vocational subjects appealed greatly to keen young men in the city and neighbouring areas of employment, and at least two were to achieve fame; Thomas Hardy, the novelist, and Albert Mansbridge, the founder of the Workers' Educational Association. Women were excluded from attendance, though a ladies department was founded in Kensington later to become King's College for Women. However good its intentions were, the college was not well placed to deal with the growing demand for classes throughout the metropolitan area, especially when the Education Act (1870) began to make its impact.

The alternative was for a voluntary body to lead the way and this eventually emerged as the London Society for the Extension of University Teaching.

[1]James Stuart, (1843–1913), regarded as the 'father of University Extension' by virtue of his pioneering lectures on astronomy delivered in 1867 to audiences recruited by the North of England Council for the Higher Education of Women. Its president was Mrs Josephine Butler to whose crusade against the Contagious Diseases Acts, Stuart gave much support; first Professor of Mechanism and Applied Mechanics at Cambridge (1875); later entered politics as Liberal MP for Hoxton, (1885–1900), and Sunderland, (1906–10).

At this distance of time it is difficult to establish how the idea of the society first emerged, though some clue is afforded by the oral evidence G. J. Goschen[1] (its first president) gave before the City Livery Companies Commission in 1884 – 'there was some institution in the metropolis that applied to the Cambridge syndicate asking them to help them in London but on that being done, there was a number of gentlemen who met in London and thought they could make similar arrangements in London to those that Cambridge had made for the provincial towns'. He was possibly referring to a meeting on 10 May 1875 at the Royal Institution 'of noblemen and gentlemen', to consider 'the best mode of extending to London the benefits of the Cambridge University Extension Scheme'. This resulted in the formation of an executive committee, on 10 June, that was to organise a very large and influential meeting in the Mansion House with the Lord Mayor in the chair. Next day *The Times* wrote expansively 'this represents a germ of a movement which may ultimately extend and organise the whole of higher education of the country. Most of us can remember the day when the two Universities (Oxford and Cambridge) were regarded as overgrown and almost obsolete corporations possessing great funds which were applied with great extravagance to the exclusive education of the aristocratic and wealthy class in this country.'

From these auspicious beginnings an executive committee emerged to set about the practicalities of translating words into action, especially in securing financial support and an active membership. The immediate task was the incorporation of the London Society for the Extension of University Teaching, as it was to be styled, under the Companies Act (1867). The principal agents in these negotiations were A. Morley, MP (brother of Samuel Morley) and Walter Leaf, and at long last the LSEUT was fully registered on 12 January 1876 at the total cost of £61 16s 10d.

As with all important voluntary organisations the London Society was bound to establish a council with influential members, shortly to be headed by HRH Prince Leopold (Queen Victoria's fourth and youngest son). A letter exists from his secretary asserting 'it will give him great pleasure to

---

[1]G. J. Goschen, (1831–1901), joined his father's business, and later became governor of the Bank of England at 27. Entered the House of Commons in 1863, and held various offices including president of the Poor Law Board, First Lord of the Admiralty and Chancellor of Exchequer. Lord Rector of Aberdeen and Edinburgh Universities, and Chancellor of Oxford University; created viscount in 1901.

be associated in the scheme for Extension of University Education in London: but before giving you a definite answer he must lay the matter before the Queen'. Approval was given as was a donation of fifty guineas.

At the first general meeting of the LSEUT at the Mansion House on 13 March 1876 an impressive council of 22 members was elected, consisting not only of aristocrats, but of important figures in the educational world – James Bryce, W. B. Carpenter (registrar of the University of London), Francis Galton, Samuel Morley, and Sir Charles Reed (chairman of the London School Board). In an earlier note to Goschen, declining his invitation to join the council, Henry Fawcett had stressed the importance of having women members and had made some suggestions.[1] The first appointments which took note of Fawcett's remarks were Mrs William Grey (hon. organising secretary of the Women's Educational Union), Miss Mary Gurney, (committee member of the same body) and the Dowager Lady Stanley of Alderley (member of the Council of Girton College). Representatives were also appointed from the nine leading educational bodies in the metropolis – Bedford College, Birkbeck Institution, City of London College, the College for Men and Women, King's College, the London Institution, Queen's College, the Royal Institution, and the Working Men's College.

The president of LSEUT until his retirement in 1885 was the Rt Hon. G. J. Goschen, eventually to finish his parliamentary career as Chancellor of the Exchequer. Not a word of his interests in the university extension movement is mentioned in his two-volume biography by Sir Arthur Elliott, published in 1911. However, in the *Dictionary of National Biography*, there is a reference which clearly indicates his immense contribution to LSEUT's well-being 'From its initiation in 1879 (sic) Goschen was a vigorous supporter of the movement for extension of University Teaching in London and for many years he gave great assistance to the movement'.

In its early days LSEUT had to tread a wary path – the two established organisations, University College and King's College, were concerned about likely competition; there are also on record the doubts of one influential person, the Dean of St Pauls. Having been invited to support LSEUT, he

[1]These were Lady Stanley, Miss Chessar of the London School Board, Mrs Grey or her sister Miss Shirreff and Miss Gurney ('a capital worker'). In a PS he added Mrs W. Malleson 'who has done much to make the Croydon School Board one of the most efficient in the country'.

wrote to Goschen 'I am not without apprehension that the movement may
not be an unmixed good. I should be afraid that it would have a tendency
to condense and precipitate in raw and unprepared minds a good deal of
loose thinking which goes on especially at Oxford among the younger
men among whom, I suppose, lecturers will be mainly sought.' To temper,
as it were, this sharp judgment, he conceded 'but Cambridge is steadier and
equally energetic'.

There was some slight difficulty in securing the appointment of members to
LSEUT's joint board of representatives from Oxford, Cambridge and London.
As the board was to nominate lecturers, appoint examiners and generally to
advise on educational matters, a strong membership was essential. In
response to Goschen's letter to the Senate of the University of London the
matter was put to the vote at its meeting on 14 June 1876 when ten senators
were in favour and five against nominating three members. Why, one
wonders, did Lord Overstone, the Dean of Lincoln, the Master of Rolls,
Mr Lowe, and Dr Williamson prove so unhelpful? How did Robert Lowe
square this negative approach with his often quoted assertion that 'we must
educate our masters?' After some delay at the other two universities, the
joint board was eventually established in 1878 and now took an active
interest in the society's academic matters.

Modest office accommodation was secured at the Royal Asiatic Society's
address in Albemarle Street, W1, where LSEUT was to stay until 1886 when it
moved to larger premises at Charterhouse. The staff in these early days
was small, and included a secretary, Ernest Myers, who worked without a
salary for three years. The first reference to office expenses was in 1877
when postage, stationery, a clerk's salary, etc, are listed as £27 18s 0d out
of a total budget of £1,307 19s 11d. By 1881, Myers was being paid £250
a year. The arrival of R. D. Roberts[1] as secretary in 1885, a post he held
until his return to Cambridge in 1894, coincided with a rapid growth in the
society's affairs, both in terms of income and expenditure and the number of
classes organised. Staff expanded to meet these needs and by the 1890s
LSEUT was a thriving enterprise.

[1] R. D. Roberts, (1851–1911), university lecturer in Geology, Cambridge, 1884; secretary,
LSEUT, 1885–94; secretary of the Syndicate of Local Lectures and Examinations, Cambridge,
1894–1902; University Extension Registrar, 1902–11; secretary, Gilchrist Trust, 1899;
he was organising the first Congress of Empire Universities (1912) at the time of his
death.

There is an interesting sidelight on administrative procedures in the council's minute book when a report on the office staff was approved (28 September 1896). By this time Roberts had been appointed secretary to the Cambridge Syndicate and had been succeeded by C. W. Kimmins[1] an inspector with the Technical Education Board of the London County Council who still retained his interests in this field, being permitted to spend four half days a week working for the board, 'principally visiting polytechnics'. Otherwise he was at his office every day, usually in the morning 'Sometimes a few minutes is all the time he need spend on the work; sometimes he is there through the day'. Besides general supervision of the work of the society, 'raising money and starting new centres' were regarded as the secretary's main tasks, he was especially concerned with 'keeping his eye upon men at the Universities likely to make good lecturers'.

There was also by this time an assistant secretary, P. M. Wallace (later to become Secretary to the Senate of the new reorganised University of London in 1901). As well as attending to office routine he visited centres, three to four times a week in term time, mainly in the afternoon. Then returning to the office he was back at his desk – 'the 5 o'clock post, and at busy times, the 8 pm post need much attention' – an interesting commentary on the postal services at the end of the nineteenth century.

Organising the Work

The success of the new movement, as at Cambridge, was clearly dependent upon initiative and enterprise in the formation of local committees responsible for organising courses staffed by the society's lecturers. Fees were collected by the committee to cover, as far as possible, the expenses of the lecturer, and also the cost of publicity and accommodation. It was suggested that there were three different types of person likely to attend: (a) persons of leisure of both sexes; (b) clerks and young women employed during the day and (c) workmen especially of the artisan classes.

Fees proposed for these three groups were (a) £1 1s 0d for a course of twelve lectures, (b) 7s 6d, and (c) 5s. There were often higher charges for afternoon classes, compared with those payable for evening classes.

[1]C. W. Kimmins, (died 1948), science master, Leys School, Cambridge; staff lecturer at Cambridge; inspector of science teaching, Technical Education Board, LCC; secretary, LSEUT, 1895; chief inspector of technical education, 1900, and chief inspector, LCC, 1904–23; member of Senate, and of the Extension Board.

The essential features of the new movement are now regarded as common-place, but in 1876 they were clearly novel and unlike the traditional teaching practices at the university. 'The Society's work consists of courses of weekly lectures, each lecture occupies one hour, and is followed by class-intruction and advice as to text-books and means of effectual study. A printed syllabus is distributed to the students and questions are set at each lecture to be answered in writing at home and submitted to the lecturer for correction and comment. At the end of each course an examination (in writing) is held, which is not compulsory.'

A modest programme of seven terminal classes was launched during the autumn term 1876, as follows:

LONDON INSTITUTION
Political Economy, H. H. Asquith
Astronomy, H. McCann
English Constitutional History, E. Robertson

BIRKBECK INSTITUTION
Astronomy, H. McCann

WORKING MEN'S COLLEGE
Electricity and Magnetism, J. E. H. Gordon

CITY OF LONDON COLLEGE
History and Political Philosophy, F. W. Maitland

WIMBLEDON
Political Economy, H. H. Asquith

This programme involved the expenditure of £238 6s od (£210 on lecturers' fees), whilst receipts from students' fees amounted to £75 5s 12d, £22 5s 8d came from guaranteed contributions from three of the centres, leaving £139 8s 4d to be disbursed from LSEUT's funds, based on private subscriptions and donations. Throughout its existence this was the financial basis of its operations; student fees, the local committee's contribution, up to a third of any deficit (and if it ever happened the retention of two thirds of any surplus) with LSEUT providing up to two-thirds of any deficit and receiving one third of any surplus.

Having established itself as a working proposition, LSEUT steadily gained support and reputation, as the following table indicates:

Year	No. of Centres	No. of Courses Sessional Terminal		Lectures	Entries (i.e. enrolments)
Oct–Dec					
1876	5	—	7	77	139
1881	19	—	43	473	2,489
1886	32	—	61	671	5,084
1891–92	53	20	70	1,260	11,697
1896–97	63	35	55	1,463	14,150
1901–02	59	46	57	1,754	15,407

The statistics provide no indication of average attendance, and for this reason it is difficult to judge the work in terms of today's standards. A realistic figure would be the numbers attending the class after lectures, these statistics were produced for the autumn term 1881, but thereafter are irregular, and thus make it difficult to compare results over a period of years.

Year	Entries	Average attendance at the lecture	Average attendance at the class	Average No. of weekly papers	Certificates awarded terminally
Oct–Dec 1881	1,619	—	734	305	122
1886	5,084	3,748	2,020	806	482
1891–92	11,697	—	—	1,729	1,287
1901–02	15,407	—	—	2,728	2,257

Imperfect as these statistics are, they nevertheless demonstrate the considerable success achieved by the society, essentially a voluntary body. LSEUT was clearly responding, especially in suburban areas, to a growing demand for adult education of good quality. This was influenced by various factors – growing public enlightenment, the impact of new technologies, the steady increase in the number of alert, literate members of the working classes, and the zest for higher education amongst women.

Organising university extension lectures became yet another outlet for Victorian philanthropy, with the important difference that, unlike other contemporary charities, the local organisers were also keen members of the classes they organised. The local centre and its committee were anxious to secure the support of persons of influence in their neighbourhood, clergy, teachers and other patrons of both the middle- and working-class origin. In his evidence to the City Livery Companies Commission, Goschen was at pains to stress the wide appeal of the movement by listing the occupational background of some local centre secretaries, for example, Peckham – lawyer's clerk; Battersea – master in middle-class school; West Ham – clerk to the local board; Croydon – tradesman in the city; and Toynbee Hall – working bookbinder.

Without doubt the most important centre during LSEUT's existence was Toynbee Hall, where under the powerful influence of its warden, S. A. Barnett, an impressive programme of courses was arranged from 1884 onwards. Asquith once referred to Toynbee Hall as a 'social laboratory', an apt description of the innovation and imagination that characterised its many activities.

As early as the autumn term 1877, four classes had been had in the unlikely venue of the dissecting theatre at the London Hospital. There was therefore a tradition of educational enterprise in this area of Tower Hamlets, but with a brand new building, and with active support of keen young men from Oxford and Cambridge taking up residence at Toynbee Hall, the work rapidly expanded. Hundreds of manual workers, probably in larger pro- portion than have ever since attended university adult classes in the London area, were given a solid grounding in economics, literature, history, elec- tricity, biology and other subjects at Toynbee Hall. At the peak of its in- fluence Toynbee Hall spread its activities to surrounding areas, providing classes at Poplar, Millwall and Limehouse. To take a sample year, 1895–96, when this activity was at its peak, the average attendance at the eleven university extension courses at Toynbee Hall was 668, and 483 at the seven courses at the outlying centres, with nearly 100 students taking the relevant examinations. Nobody could complain about the fees at these new working-class centres – sixpence a course or one penny a lecture.

In addition to this intellectual activity, often regarded by Barnett as the nucleus of a future East London University, there were many other attrac- tions for the less academically inclined – club meetings, debates, reading parties, Saturday popular lectures and smoking conferences. No wonder then, that he could speak of himself as not only 'a head of an educational institute' but also as 'a director of enthusiasm, disciplined for the service of East London'.

Toynbee Hall was clearly in a class of its own – but what were the circum- stances in other centres? Some like Canning Town and Stratford tried hard to emulate its achievements, supported by the enterprising West Ham Borough Council which provided financial help under the Local Taxation Act (1890). This enabled councils to give grants in aid to technical education, more specifically for 'instruction in the principles of science and art as applied to industry'.

Other centres found it much more difficult to achieve a social mix in their classes though this was not for the want of effort. Bromley, for example, commenced its activities in 1887; with an annual subscription of £1 1s 0d which entitled the holder to four tickets, two for the Michaelmas term and two for Lent. Single course tickets were 15s for afternoon sessions, and 7s 6d for those held in the evening. 'Teachers, governesses, National and Board school teachers, also companions and shop assistants were admitted half price', whilst 'artisans in receipt of a weekly wage were charged 1s for an evening ticket'. Yet the secretary had to assert (*University Extension Journal,* January 1890) 'The proportion of working men is surprisingly small and it must be confessed that at present they have as a class been quite untouched by the Movement, in spite of consistent efforts made to lead them through the various agencies – Working men's clubs, Mutual Improvement Societies etc, established for their benefit in the neighbourhood.' Bromley was essentially a middle-class area and, given the social divisions there and elsewhere, it was perhaps expecting too much that the university extension movement could succeed in breaking down class barriers.

PROBLEMS OF FINANCE

It was the perennial shortage of funds that acted as the main brake on LSEUT's activities, requiring unremitting efforts by its officers and, above all, by Goschen, to maintain a state of solvency. In the early days it was the subscription of 55 members (£138 15s 0d) that kept things going, a state of affairs that was regarded as unpromising.

A public appeal for additional funds was launched in 1879 which brought in £736 5s from individuals and commercial firms. There was also the first instalment of generous help from the Gilchrist Educational Fund (£100), supplemented in 1881 by 100 guineas from the Clothworkers Company. As the years went by a few more public bodies and private individuals made donations. Life membership was fifty guineas and the annual subscription was two guineas. This enabled LSEUT to express a certain degree of pride in its financial situation, as an extract from one of its reports show:

	Paid to Lecturers	Received from Centres	Net amount paid by Society	As a percentage of Gross Expenditure
1876	210 0s 0d	98 17s 8d	111 2s 4d	52.8
1880	1,167 4s 0d	877 3s 6d	290 0s 6d	24.8
1883	1,330 0s 0d	1,189 6s 9d	140 13s 3d	10.5

Goschen, good financier as he was, was constantly on the lookout for additional funds, which explains his eagerness to present evidence to the City Livery Companies Commission in 1884. He stressed how the LSEUT worked with 'very great economy' and how it might have to suspend operations. He listed the contributions so far received from the City – 100 guineas from the Clothworkers Company and 50 guineas from the Court of Common Council. He hoped that more would be forthcoming – £2–4,000 pa was the sum he had in mind. 'Do you think,' asked the chairman 'if you had this sum secured to you that it would not send you all to sleep?' Not a very generous question it might be thought. 'Certainly not' replied Goschen 'I can say we have not been asleep so far'. 'You have had to work for your money?' Goschen replied positively and went on to explain how he had written nearly 600 letters to his personal friends for financial help. Although the list of subscribers lengthened as a result of these endeavours, little extra cash was immediately forthcoming from the City. A novel fund-raising appeal was made in the autumn of 1884 when publishing houses in London were invited 'to support the organisation for the Extension of University Teaching, which, has, during late years, done so much to create a love of literature and to promote the study of books amongst London men and women'. Twelve publishers responded to this plea by donating £77 5s 0d and paying annual subscriptions of £55 8s 0d. By 1890 more money was forthcoming from the City, with £910 being received from the Gilchrist Trustees, the Mitchell City of London Charity, the Court of Common Council and seven City Livery Companies – a useful amount, but still small compared with the sum of £3,115 14s disbursed by local centres. As most of this money was only granted on a short-term basis LSEUT could never relax its efforts to secure its financial viability.

As with other Victorian charities, the Mansion House was the occasional venue for fund-raising efforts. In the spring of 1891, Goschen met the masters of the leading City Livery Companies and appealed to their generosity – with modest success it would appear, only £473 15s being donated.

By this time State aid was becoming a topic of urgent discussion amongst other universities providing extension courses, and LSEUT received an invitation from Cambridge towards the end of 1893 to join a deputation to the Chancellor of the Exchequer. Goschen poured cold water on this idea, asserting that 'the present conditions of financial affairs make it quite impossible for the Chancellor of the Exchequer to give favourable consideration to the request'. He then stressed the undesirability of approaching the Chancellor 'with the certainty of a refusal', and the council agreed with this view, based, no doubt, on Goschen's parliamentary insight. In view of this situation there was no option but to press for further private funds and the secretary was instructed, at its meeting on 28 February 1895, to prepare 'a list of City Companies and the names of friends through whom they might be approached'. He was also to call on bankers, companies and publishers. As a result of dispatching some 2,000 circulars, £140 5s was promised in donations and £34 12s in subscriptions 'for lectures to artisans'.

LSEUT never lost sight of the need to carry on its activities in these areas, and from time to time was assisted by the Gilchrist Trustees and the City Parochial Trustees. One noteworthy enterprise which resulted from this income, first arranged in 1887, were the 'People's Lectures', free of charge, and often attracting large audiences.

This type of course received further encouragement when, as a result of the Local Taxation Act (1890), money became available for technical education. Under these auspices both the West Ham Town Council and the Technical Education Board of the London County Council joined LSEUT in organising courses. At Canning Town, during the spring term 1892, 387 enrolled for a free course on astronomy and at Stratford Town Hall, 800 for a similar venture on the 'Chemistry of Everyday Life', both supported by the West Ham authority. In the next session 1893–94, five courses were organised with the LCC at Deptford, Fulham, Poplar, Shoreditch, and Wandsworth. These were given by Professor V. B. Lewes[1] of the Royal Naval College on

---

[1]Vivian B. Lewes, (1852–1915), was brought up by his uncle, the Victorian philosopher, George Henry Lewes. After holding posts in the laboratories at University College and Birkbeck Institution, he became Professor of Chemistry, Royal Naval College Greenwich 1888–1914; and vice-president of the Institution of Naval Architects; his research interests in coal-gas led to his appointment as chief gas examiner in the City of London 1893; a popular lecturer not only for LSEUT, but elsewhere, including the Royal Society of Arts where he gave the record number of over 60 lectures; died, shortly after giving a lecture on 'Explosives used in the Great War', at Mold, north Wales.

the highly popular subject the 'Chemistry of Air, Fire and Water', and attracted the considerable enrolment of 3,250. This did not exhaust his formidable stamina as Lewes repeated the course twice more during the session at Hornsey and Stratford to audiences totalling 1,160.

RECRUITING THE LECTURERS

How lecturers were recruited by LSEUT is not immediately clear – presumably, then as now, a number came along as a result of personal enquiry or recommendation. Standards required from applicants were high – they were to be 'of highest academic honours and thoroughly qualified for the communication of knowledge and for the stimulation of thought'. There was a steady flow of inquiries from prospective lecturers, and the ultimate decision whether or not to approve applications was left to the joint board. When the board was established in 1879, *The Times* wrote rather curiously about prospective lecturers 'The young scientific and legal luminary who is despatched from Oxford or Cambridge to contact listening Londoners may find it less easy than he expects to come up to the demands of his audience. He will be dealing not with the semi-rustic population of a provincial town, not with an obedient band of college pupils who feel him a better master than themselves of the accustomed text books of the place'. What type of audience he might expect was not specified, but the extension lecturer even in those days clearly had to be on his toes, especially in London.

Young men down from Oxford or Cambridge were often regarded as suitable material. Asquith, having completed his legal training, gave five courses whilst in his mid-twenties and then moved to a different occupation, as did other lecturers including Oliver Lodge, R. E. Prothero, Karl Pearson and F. Y. Edgeworth. These and other names appear for a few sessions in LSEUT's annual arrangements and then disappear.

The records of the joint board are sparse, but there is a minute book which contains some interesting references to the lecturing staff. To take the meeting held on 20 February 1893 as an example, the board instructed the secretary to inform nineteen applicants (including H. G. Wells, then 26) that there were no vacancies for teaching the subjects they offered. However 'the academical qualifications' of eight other persons were accepted and it was agreed that they should give a trial lecture. How these were arranged is obscure, though one of these eight was eventually given an opportunity of delivering two lectures at Homerton Training College, Cambridge, which were considered 'fairly satisfactory', and (as is still often the case) the applicant was told to get more experience.

Sometimes prospective lecturers were more likely to be accepted by the joint board if they could persuade an established centre to invite them to lecture. Such was the enterprise of Percival Gaskell who offered the 'History of Italian Painting', and then in response to this advice was recruited by the Marylebone Centre. After a favourable report had been received about his work he joined the ranks of extension lecturers, enjoying this position for another forty years until his death in 1934.

In the last decade of the century a few applications were received from female lecturers, including Miss Helen Denby[1] of Newnham College, Cambridge. She was clearly well qualified (first class honours in Mental and Moral Tripos and Cobden Scholar), and moreover, Essex Hall (a flourishing centre off the Strand and probably a little advanced in its ideas) wanted her to lecture on the 'Methods of Social Reform'.

There was clearly some dispute at the joint board's meeting on 13 November 1894 when her application was being considered and it was only after some discussion that she was appointed for this particular course. At its next meeting a letter was received by the joint board from H. S. Foxwell (Professor of Political Economy, University College, London and representative of the University of Cambridge) resigning his membership, a step he took because of his difference of view from the majority of the joint board on the question of appointing women lecturers. Despite this event, Miss Denby gave her course (though the title was changed to the 'Principles of Social Development') to an audience of over 70 students. Her name appeared on one or two other occasions in LSEUT's programme, but there is no inkling whether Foxwell was for or against all female lecturers for he had earlier written enthusiastically about Mrs Millicent Fawcett (page 17).

A small cadre of lecturers were to dedicate the best years of their lives to university extension lecturing and to achieve considerable fame and, presumably, a fairly steady income. At this time a course of twelve lectures was

[1]Helen Denby, (1860–1925), married the philosopher Bernard Bosanquet with whom she had worked in the Charity Organisation Society; member of the Royal Commission on the Poor Laws; and author of *Social Work in London* (1914).

paid for at the rate of £30, though popular lecturers could expect £60, and this when £1 was the weekly wage of many manual workers, and income tax at 7*d* in the pound.

Perhaps the most outstanding lecturer was Philip H. Wicksteed[1], who was employed by LSEUT, from 1887 until 1916, as well as being on the books of Oxford and Cambridge. At the peak of his abilities he undertook a programme of lectures which today would be regarded as likely to tax most lecturers' physical, if not their intellectual, resources. The session 1896–97 is a good example of his stamina when his programme was as follows:

MICHAELMAS TERM
Bloomsbury: 'The theory of earning and spending' (part ii); Chelsea: Wordsworth; Croydon: 'The theory of earning and spending' (part i); Regent Street Polytechnic: 'Dante'.

LENT TERM
Bushey Heath: 'Wordsworth'; Chelsea: 'Dante'; Chislehurst: 'Dante' (part ii); Regent Street Polytechnic: 'Dante' (part ii).

SUMMER TERM
Chelsea: 'Dante's *Convito*'; Croydon: 'Currency and finance'; Regent Street Polytechnic: 'Dante's *Convito*';

In addition his employment with other universities took him into the provinces; Michaelmas Term Dover: 'Dante'; Leicester: 'Dante'; Lent Term Dover: 'Dante'; Brighton: 'Dante's *Purgatorio*'; and finally at Leeds, two terms, yet again on Dante.

His biographer tells us that 'he held spellbound audiences which became in reality congregations by a fusion of documented scholarship unusual in any pulpit with a prophetic fire rare in any university'. As well as presenting Dante to many different audiences, he achieved great fame both as a writer and lecturer on economics 'crowded with homely illustrations from practical life' especially in his courses on 'Getting and Spending'. Not only was he

---

[1]P. H. Wicksteed, (1844–1927), Unitarian minister, Taunton, Dukinfield and at the Little Portland Street Chapel, London (1874–1922); university extension lecturer, London and the provinces (1887–1918) on economics and Dante ('the most acceptable and accepted interpreter of Dante to the cultivated laity of England,' *pace* his biographer, C. H. Herford); warden of University Hall, Gordon Square, (planned as the 'Toynbee Hall of liberal theology'); of outstanding presence and physique, 'at 80 could outwalk and outstride most younger men'.

a masterful presenter of economics, we have it on the authority of Professor Lionel Robbins (as he then was, writing in *Economica*, November 1930) that there were few economists 'who have done more to bring economics as a science into relation with life as a whole', than Wicksteed.

There were other lecturers of similar calibre, though in different disciplines, during these early years of the movement, including J. Churton Collins[1] and Vivian B. Lewes. Collins was employed by LSEUT from 1880–1907, during which time he delivered some 3,000 lectures. During session 1895–96 he gave seven courses during the Michaelmas term, the same number during Lent and five during the summer term.

When Asquith introduced Collins at the first lecture of his course on the 'Beginnings of English Literature' at Gresham College, Michaelmas 1892 (215 enrolments), he asserted 'I do not believe that the subject of English Literature could be handled by any more competent man in the whole of Great Britain'.

He must be one of the few lecturers to enjoy royal patronage. In his course on 'Leaders in Elizabethan Literature' at the Kew and Richmond Centre (average attendance 90) his students included the Duchess of Teck and her daughter, Princess May. They attended 'all the lectures but three, but did not incline to do any paper work' (extract from Collins' class report, 1891). A few years later this episode was to be embroidered into a story which implied that the royal students were, like their fellows, avid readers and writers of weekly papers, 'Princess May took notes, wrote papers and was as eager to receive the lecturer's corrections and marks as any of us, her classmates'. (*University Extension Journal*, 1910, quoting *Manchester Guardian*.)

It is hard to imagine how Lewes achieved such enormous popularity and following as a lecturer on scientific topics. Yet we have it on the authority of Albert Mansbridge[2] who attended his course on the 'Chemistry of Air,

[1] J. Churton Collins, (1848–1908), after studying history and law at Oxford, gave his first university extension lectures at Brixton, 1880 'a veritable missionary of the humane letters' (Stephen Potter), thereafter in great demand as lecturer; first holder of chair in English literature at Birmingham in 1904.

[2] Albert Mansbridge, CH, (1876–1952), boy copyist in the Inland Revenue; clerk in the Goldsmiths' and Silversmiths' Company and the Co-operative Wholesale Society; cashier, Co-operative Permanent Building Society; founded the WEA 1903, the National Central Library, and the Seafarers' Education Service; amongst his books *The Trodden Road* (1940) is especially relevant.

Fire and Water' that it was 'a most attractive and exciting course'. In spite of his youthful age of fifteen Mansbridge was properly enrolled as a student, gaining a distinction certificate in the examination at the end of the course and a prize which consisted of 'a free gift of my photograph by a local photographer'. (Incidentally, the examiner's report indicated that Mansbridge was awarded 85 out of 100 marks.)

At this time lectures on scientific and technical subjects, amounting to about half the total programme of courses, were very popular – this was the age of electricity and rapid advances in various technologies. Lewes and others were skilled in delivering courses to meet this demand and were also keen to involve their students in practical work. In one of his syllabuses 'Practical Chemistry and Manipulation' Lewes wrote 'I shall show students how to build up and make for themselves all the apparatus necessary for the preparation of the commoner gases and instead of using expensive materials, I shall point out how, by the expenditure of a few shillings and the utilisation of empty pickle bottles, old oil flasks and such simple appliances, they may obtain the power of manipulation and experimenting which, as a rule, is only obtained by expensive courses of instruction in regular laboratories'.

The time expended in preparing a university extension course must have been considerable – syllabuses were often miniature textbooks and works of considerable scholarship. The quantity of weekly essays received by some lecturers must frequently have reached great proportions. During session 1895–96 Lewes would appear, from the records, to have received nearly 1,800 papers, produced at weekly intervals. It is difficult to judge their character or length but they required careful assessment and lecturers sometimes sub-contracted this task to junior markers. Occasionally the arrangements came unstuck and if news of irregularities reached the joint board, acrimonious correspondence might ensue. This happened to Lewes in connection with his work during session 1894–95 when it was noted that his assistant had been marking papers submitted by the class at Poplar in a 'disgracefully careless fashion'. The excuse offered was pressure of time to ensure the prompt despatch of the marks to the society's office. The joint board were firm in their attitude to this misdemeanour and asked Lewes to make a weekly inspection of the marking arrangements. Lewes was not amused and his resignation was handed in by return of post. Presumably there must have been a reconciliation as Lewes applied to be reinstated a few weeks later.

The first female lecturer for LSEUT was Mrs Sophie Bryant[1] who was invited by the Camden Road Centre during the spring term of 1885 to give a course on 'Moral Ideals'. There was an enrolment of 82 for the course, and 'the fact that the average attendance was seventy proved that the lectures were highly appreciated'. She must have been a successful lecturer as she was persuaded to continue during the summer with a class on Aristotle's Ethics.

Another distinguished lecturer was Mrs Millicent Fawcett (wife of Henry Fawcett, MP, and later an eloquent suffragist). She gave two courses in 1892 at Canonbury and Marylebone on 'Problems of Poverty' to large audiences made up of voluntary workers for the Charity Organisation Society, poor law guardians and others active in what would now be called social work. Eight students from the Marylebone class took the examination set by Professor Foxwell. He wrote enthusiastically about their papers 'astonishingly good with a completeness of style rarely found, they wrote as if they were discussing practical business and not mere bookwork. Unfortunately answers of such remarkable excellence as these cannot be hoped for except at long intervals'.

In view of this outstanding performance it is rather strange that Mrs Fawcett should have written in her class report 'the result is probably rather outside the aim of the University Extension Society, but it appears to me not unworthy of notice'. Did somebody in authority disapprove of this type of class or was it perhaps regarded as professional training and not to be encouraged? Whatever the reasons, the class was not repeated and courses specifically for social workers did not feature in the programme until many years later.

Sometimes lectures ran foul of LSEUT for odd reasons which on a closer inspection may well have been related to the antagonism of an individual member of the joint board. The classic case of disapproval is that of J. A. Hobson. In his autobiography, *Confessions of an Economic Heretic,* he wrote that his *Physiology of Industry* published in 1887 was opening new arguments about oversaving, 'This was the first open step in my heretical career, and I

---

[1]Sophie Bryant, (1850–1922), married at 19 and when her husband died a year later returned to her studies, eventually becoming the first woman DSc (1884, thesis topic, *Organised Character*); mathematics mistress at the North London Collegiate School, and its headmistress, 1895–1918; member of various bodies including Convocation, also first woman Convocation Senator; the London County Council's Education Committee; and the Extension Board.

did not in the least realise its momentous consequences . . . The first shock came in a refusal of the London Extension Board to allow me to offer courses of political economy'. Tawney was later to write in his contribution on Hobson's life in the *Dictionary of National Biography* 'the London University Extension Board (sic) with surprising fatuity refused to allow Hobson to lecture for it on political economy'.

Yet the facts as reported in the minutes of the universities' joint board tell a slightly different story. Some time in the late 1880s Hobson was clearly not allowed to lecture on economics, possibly at the behest of Professor Foxwell, though the embargo did not relate to his lectures on English literature. The matter came up for review at the joint board's meeting on 23 February 1893 when the minutes reported an application from Hobson to be recognised as a lecturer in economics. After discussion, it was decided that the opinions of leading economists at Oxford and Cambridge should be taken upon his syllabus and his published work. Mr Wells was asked to see Mr Phelps and Mr Rice at Oxford, and Professor Foxwell to see Professor Marshall and Dr Keynes at Cambridge. There is no indication what these enquiries revealed in terms of Hobson's scholarship or views for the minutes of the meeting held on 23 June 1893 reported that 'the opinions from Oxford were strongly in favour of recognition, whilst those from Cambridge were more doubtful'. However, Hobson's name was added to the list of lecturers on economics and he was employed from 1896 onwards.[1]

WHO WERE THE STUDENTS?

Except in general terms information about students is much more difficult to obtain – afternoon classes often recruiting a middle-class audience, with courses held at Toynbee Hall and its associated centres attracting many manual workers. LSEUT throughout its history was at great pains to recruit working-class students and eagerly reported such courses wherever they occurred. In the report for 1886 it relates the success in enlisting audiences from various wage-earning occupations, including men engaged in ship building, boiler makers, coopers, sawyers and dock labourers. One of these courses given at Poplar by G. Armitage Smith must have included a future working-class politician, Will Crooks, MP. In his biography, (G. Haw:

[1] e.g., In the Lent term 1896 at the Borough Polytechnic where 68 students enrolled for his course on 'Work and Wages'.

The Life Story of Will Crooks, MP), there is a reference to his attendance at a 'university class on Political Economy delivered in Poplar by Mr G. Armitage Smith'. This course clearly made a great impact on its members 'with the class being protracted to a late hour' and with students keenly interested 'in testing the principles of Political Economy by the facts of everyday life'.

There were a number of gifted lecturers able to attract working-class audiences, but often against odds. Many manual workers lacked sufficient basic education and the economic pressures of the times often sapped enterprise and initiative in attending courses. There was also a certain degree of apathy as was noted by perceptive observers at Toynbee Hall, for instance E. J. Urwick quoted in its annual report, 1898–99, 'A few years ago, a good University Extension Society's course was sure to attract a good audience, now the attendance will not be more than two thirds of what it was. . . . The fault, if fault it is, seems to be with the lectured and not the lecturer; the food supplied is the same, the appetitite or taste is changed.'

Most students who attended classes outside the East End were from the middle classes with a fair sprinkling of clerks and elementary school-teachers. This was corroborated in 1888 by the society's secretary, R. D. Roberts, in his evidence to the Royal Commission on a University for London. A later witness, Henry Keatley Moore, had some interesting things to say about the Croydon Centre where he was secretary 'there is no large extension class at Croydon, but we have generally one or two students (out of 100 or so) fairly coming under the denomination of superior artisans'. He went on to talk about graduates, solicitors, merchants and governesses, which led the chairman to put the point 'Several of these were evidently not persons in want of University education, because they had had it?' Back came the reply – 'unless the teaching was of a very high character such persons . . . would not have felt sufficiently interested to submit themselves to continual study'. Finally, in an attempt to impress the commission, Moore mentioned the achievements of Miss Benson, the Archbishop of Canterbury's daughter, who had produced 'some really remarkable papers' for J. Churton Collins. Dr Ball (member of the commission) was prompted to enquire further 'You would not consider an archbishop's daughter as a sample of Croydon?' Back came the egregious Mr Moore 'Certainly not, but the archbishop lives close to Croydon, and that is the reason why Miss Benson attends our classes'. He only wanted to make the point, he asserted, that the teaching was always of the very highest description.

The institution of sessional certificates in 1885, with the possibility of a certificate for continuous study, had a considerable appeal especially for pupil teachers who were given some exemption from the Queen's Scholarship examination on the basis of their certificates. The term 'continuous study' meant six awards based on not more than three subjects, each of which had to be studied over at least two successive terms, covering both literary and historical as well as scientific subjects. Bright young men in the City were also given some incentive to attend classes and take certificates as 200 firms, belonging to the London Chamber of Commerce, agreed to give preference to employees showing this enterprise. Nevertheless this must have been regarded as a modest achievement by members of LSEUT – their expectation was to remain unfulfilled, that certificates should pave the way to a university degree, even, and this was Goschen's view, if it might involve eight years' study.

Two Memorable Events

During the last decade of the LSEUT's existence there were two events which epitomised its drive and enterprise. The first was the University Extension Congress organised as LSEUT's contribution to the twenty-first anniversary of the beginnings of the work at Cambridge. Nearly 700 representatives from home and abroad met during June 1894 to consider the reports of three committees which surveyed topics of perennial interest:

(1) the future development of the university extension movement
(2) its relationship with central and local governments, and
(3) studies for university degrees.

The chancellors of the Universities of Oxford, Cambridge and London presided over the three sessions at which these reports were discussed. At the opening of the conference Lord Salisbury (Oxford) treated the delegates to an eloquent speech 'Your lectures are popular' he proclaimed 'they gather enormous classes, they are increasing in range every year, and we can do nothing more than wish for an extension of that success'. He continued in this vein, reaching the inevitable peroration, 'Be very careful before you exchange the system of lectures with elementary examinations which are healthy for the hot-house, the high-pressure system of examinations, for the purpose of obtaining degrees which gratify emulation, which are pleasant to ambition, but which involve no real conquests in the healthy salutary domain of true knowledge and intellectual progress'.

According to *The Times,* in its report on the congress, he was greeted with loud applause, though some of the audience may not have shared his reflections on the value of studies for degrees. After the splendid reception of 800 delegates and friends by the Lord Mayor at the Mansion House on the final evening there was a general feeling of achievement. 'The University Extension movement' asserted *The Times* in one of its leaders 'has no enemies, but many friends.' This was some consolation, perhaps, for those who were anxious about the future of LSEUT.

The last major event which again brought LSEUT and its work before the public eye was its summer meeting held from 30 May to 11 June 1898. Although it was intended as a celebration of its twenty-first anniversary, there must have been a certain *fin de siècle* atmosphere about the proceedings. Over a thousand tickets were issued at the not inconsiderable sum of two guineas, in exchange for which there was a feast of lectures, garden parties (at Devonshire House and Fulham Palace) and receptions. When it was all over and the final accounts settled, the LSEUT's council were agreeably surprised to learn that there was a profit of £542 14s 0d. As a reward to their hardworking and thrifty staff they voted the following sums: £60 to the secretary, £40 to the assistant secretary, £20 to the chief clerk, and to the second clerk, whose weekly wage was £1, the useful sum of £10. The balance of £412 14s 0d was invested in LCC consolidated stock producing the modest return of 2½ per cent interest. As a final act of generosity to its loyal secretary, Dr C. W. Kimmins, the council voted 100 guineas of this reserve as a parting gift just before its dissolution in July 1902.

THE LONDON SOCIETY AND UNIVERSITY REFORM

Towards the end of the century there was growing agitation for the reform of the University, inspired largely by the Association for Promoting a Teaching University in London (1884). This led to two Royal Commissions being set up to investigate the various issues that were being raised – the Selborne Commission reporting in 1888, and the far more effective Gresham Commission in 1894.

Such was the standing of LSEUT that its evidence was given serious consideration and its witnesses closely examined when they appeared before the two bodies. LSEUT was represented in 1888 by the Marquis of Ripon, Canon Westcott (though his experience was based on Cambridge), R. D. Roberts (the society's secretary) and H. Keatley Moore (secretary to the

Croydon Centre). The Marquis was examined with a fair amount of deference by Rev J. E. C. Weldon (member of the Commission) 'If I understand rightly, my Lord, the work that is now being done by the University scheme would be included in the work of the new teaching university?' The Marquis – 'Nothing would give us greater pleasure than to hand over the whole of our work to a teaching university for London'.

In his evidence Roberts gave a detailed account of LSEUT's work, indicating its appeal both to the middle-class and artisan audiences. He spoke with obvious pleasure about the centre at Ponders End, near the Swan Edison Light works, where there was an audience of about one hundred for each of two terminal courses on chemistry and electricity, the latter 'a subject which the more intelligent of the workmen were naturally anxious to follow'. As he proceeded with his evidence it was clear that LSEUT was increasingly concerned about wider opportunities for some of its students to be admitted to degree studies, with some concessions for their work in extension courses. He reflected the views of LSEUT president, Goschen, when he envisaged the possibility of Gresham College becoming a base for such activity – 'there could be no more dignified position or one more in accord with the very spirit of the foundation of Gresham College, than for the College to be constituted such an evening college, the head of the whole system and a part of the University'. He further speculated that 'a very considerable number of the 20 or 25 per cent of students taking University Extension examinations might be prepared to undertake degree studies'. When asked to give a more precise indication of the numbers likely to be involved, he must have sounded somewhat less convincing. There were 5,662 'entries' in 1887 (this was the term conventionally used in the society's statistics, equivalent to enrolments and involving a certain amount of imprecision and even inflation) – 'I have not the exact number who present themselves for examination, but the number who obtained certificates was 612'.

Having listened to the eloquence of LSEUT's witnesses and having studied its submissions, all the commission could eventually assert was that they had received 'a good deal of interesting evidence from the Society'. They also conceded that if various educational institutions in London, including LSEUT, could be co-ordinated under the direction of a university (they were still undecided about what kind of organisation it might be) then 'the cause of education in the Metropolis might gain a great impetus'.

Undaunted by this lukewarm response and the commission's unwillingness to be more positive, LSEUT's next step was to present a memorial to the

Senate. In this they urged that university extension students should be permitted to complete their study for a degree over six to eight years. To support their suggestion extracts were quoted from reports of examiners, including that on the work of candidates at the Lewisham Centre who had attended a course of physiology. 'The standard set was that of the pass examination of the Conjoint Board of the Colleges of Surgeons and Physicians, and all the candidates came fully up to that standard, whilst some of those "distinguished" would have passed the examination required in Physiology by the University of London at the first M.B.' The point was further emphasised with the assertion 'that the offer of increased facilities for education strongly stimulates and awakens the demand for it'. But their pleading fell on deaf ears.

When the Cowper Commission was eventually set up in 1893 to tackle the still unresolved problems of university reorganisation, fortunately for LSEUT one of the commissioners was Canon Browne. As a former member of its council, he was well acquainted with its achievements and expectations. Once again, witnesses testified to the good work being done. Collins referred to the 'very large and increasing number of men and women who are not only eager but hope for advanced instruction of a liberal kind'. W. Ramsay, Professor of Chemistry, University College, London, on the other hand, was somewhat lukewarm when he asserted that 'University Extension was good work, but not University work' and that it lacked 'sufficient provision for sequence and co-ordination of study' – a view shared by Canon Barnett in his plea for 'a much more regular and continuous system of teaching'. From the LSEUT's secretary came the opinion that it was more difficult to prepare university extension lectures than college lectures (Roberts had taught geology at Cambridge).

Once again there was pressure for wider facilities for degree studies. The chairman, 'Do you think that a working man occupied during the working hours every day really could take a degree which would be of value?'. Roberts, 'Certainly, and I believe by lengthening the period of such study and by reducing the amount of final examination that he had to undergo to what the University might itself conclude was a proportionate quantity, you would give a degree and that degree would be taken and would mean as good an amount of mental cultivation as is practically got by any person who takes a degree at any university'. Roberts then went on to declare that he would not regard eight years out of the question for such study, and then came the final apologia 'We believe the offer of a degree would be a powerful lever to improve and increase the efficiency of the work done.'

When the commission's report eventually appeared it included the modest opinion that 'the University Extension system deserved the encouragement of the University' and recommended the appointment of 'a standing board to encourage and extend this work in London and the suburbs.'

A few more years were to elapse before the passing of the University of London Act (1898). LSEUT must have wondered about its future, as it was not until October in the following year that it received a letter from the commission set up to implement the Act. They still entertained the expectation of becoming an established department of the University, possibly with degree granting facilities – but this was dispelled by the sentence 'the Commission do not feel justified in treating the Society as a Public Educational Institution within the meaning of the Act'. As a consolation, there was reference to 'the appointment of a standing committee to advise the Senate upon the means best adapted to encourage work of the kind done by your Society'.

THE LAST YEARS OF THE LONDON SOCIETY

This report was final, and for the next three years the business of winding up the society's affairs went on at a leisurely pace. Sometimes doubts and disappointments must have been expressed at the council's meetings when decisions about the transfer were usually prefaced in the minutes by the words 'after some discussion'. The bridge was ultimately crossed at the meeting on 17 July 1902 when three resolutions were eventually passed:

(1) that the society be dissolved on 1 October 1902;
(2) that its activities be transferred to the board to promote the extension of university teaching in accordance with two previous Senate resolutions (these provided for the take over of existing arrangements for lecturers and lectures and for the maintenance of LSEUT policy of helping poor centres and encouraging liberal studies in polytechnics and technical institutions);
(3) that as far as possible the university extension method of work be encouraged and maintained.

At the meeting of LSEUT on 26 July a letter, received from the Bishop of Bristol (formerly Canon Browne), was read which contained the final glowing sentence (not a model of literary elegance) 'Indeed it is not too much to say that to the work of the Society, the maturing of the impulse towards a Teaching University was in no small part due'. This was perhaps its major achievement – that it had played a major part in the evolution of the reorganised University of London. Nevertheless disappointments were often expressed that 'a great Central College for evening students', as envisaged by R. D. Roberts, had not been established.

TWENTY-FIVE YEARS OF ACHIEVEMENT

If there were no University Extension College as a memorial to the enterprise of the London Society, as had been created at Exeter and elsewhere, there were other successes. Within the brief space of 25 years LSEUT had built up a network of flourishing centres where 'a high degree of educational thoroughness' (Roberts) was achieved.

Many of the courses were attended by middle-class audiences, a fact disparagingly referred to by various critics, as if LSEUT was limited in its view of the scope of adult education. Time and time again its organisers were acutely aware of the need to recruit what were variously called artisans or weekly wage-earners. And to encourage such work they made repeated efforts to secure financial support which, in spite of the opulence of late-Victorian London, was only grudgingly forthcoming with the honourable exceptions of some City charities, especially the City Parochial Charities and the Gilchrist Trustees. The educational needs of working-class students represented a low priority. Moreover the response from public authorities was limited to the Technical Education Board of the London County Council and the West Ham Council, both of which supported courses under the broad heading of 'technical instruction'. Finally, after the publication of the report of the Departmental Committee on Pupil Teachers (1898), the London School Board during the last years of its existence supported sessional courses at its various pupil-teacher centres.

In 1895 a petition, signed by nearly 500 influential persons in public affairs, the Church and education, was presented to the Chancellor of the Exchequer. It made a plea for £6,000 a year to be allocated in equal shares to the four university extension authorities, the Oxford Delegacy, the Cambridge Syndicate, the London Society and the Victoria Committee (at Manchester), and to the two University Extension Colleges at Reading and Exeter. The arguments presented were cogent. 'It is of real importance that, with a view to the training of good citizens courses of teaching should be provided in historical, literary, economic and other non-technical subjects. The need for a comprehensive system of education for those above school age is becoming every year more urgent, and every improvement in secondary education renders more imperative the creation of a national system of higher education giving facilities to those engaged in the ordinary occupations of life for definite and systematic study.' It is a commentary on national priorities that nearly 50 years were to elapse before a comprehensive Education Act was passed to tackle these challenges.

To carry out its tasks LSEUT was fortunate enough to enlist the services of teachers who were a source of inspiration to their students. Some even made a more lasting impression by giving their subjects a modern touch. Collins, for example, was largely responsible for transforming the study of English literature, and confidently expected to be appointed as first holder of the chair in the subject at Oxford in 1887. But, in spite of support from several influential persons, including Gladstone, Matthew Arnold and Benjamin Jowett, he was not appointed mainly because of the popular success of his (extension) lecturing[1]. Eventually Birmingham appointed Collins to a chair in 1904 thus redeeming Oxford's failure.

But it was in the field of science that major innovations occurred. Was it because Roberts was a scientist (first class honours in Natural Science Tripos 1874) that there was an expanding programme of courses in scientific topics? Perhaps another explanation might be the absence of alternative provision until the emergence of polytechnics and technical colleges in the last decade of the nineteenth century. Whatever the reasons, there were large audiences for lecturers of the calibre of Lewes, a great pioneer of science education, who 'undoubtedly contributed to the success of many of our technical institutes, for the number of students induced to follow up their preliminary work at his lectures by systematic study was indeed large' (*Journal of the Chemical Society, Transactions,* 1916).

Public examinations were essentially a Victorian invention and, after the establishment of the Civil Service Commission (1855) and the Cambridge Local Examinations' Syndicate, they played an increasing rôle in a rapidly changing society. London had its matriculation, but the regulations were onerous for most adult students who wanted some evidence of intellectual achievement. LSEUT catered for these growing aspirations and, as the figures indicate, did much to satisfy this demand: 1879, 57 certificates; 1890, 1,349; and 1902, 2,257. Although its aspiration to become involved in degree work

---

[1]Stephen Potter: *The Muse in Chains: a Study in Education,* 1937, p 188.

was to remain unfulfilled, LSEUT could well feel satisfied with this record. It demonstrated that adult students were anxious to take written tests and that they could achieve good standards of work, a firm basis for the diploma scheme to be launched in 1909.

By way of a postscript to the crowded 25 years of LSEUT's history, reference may be made to an earlier event. This was the meeting held at the Mansion House, February 1879, to inaugurate the joint board with its representatives from Oxford, Cambridge and London. After an eloquent speech from Gladstone, Prince Leopold then addressed the large gathering of leading personalities, from the City, Church, and the educational world. 'In no city' he asserted 'is there to be found more intellectual capacity in an untutored state than in London'. To remedy this state of ignorance, he commended the work of the London Society which could provide, through local committees, 'a network of well-ordered knowledge and elevated thought'. Had Prince Leopold enjoyed more robust health (he died at the age of 30) he might have played a notable part in the advancement of higher education – at least he is to be remembered for his patronage of the London Society, for having opened two buildings (Firth College, Sheffield, 1879, and University College, Nottingham, 1881, both closely associated with the university extension movement), and having laid the foundation stone for the new Birkbeck Institution in 1883.

At the time when Prince Leopold spoke, elementary education had just been assumed as a public commitment, and it was not until 1890 that it was made compulsory up to the age of ten. There was therefore plenty of work to be done in late Victorian London. With all the drive and energy of a pioneering body LSEUT had set about its many tasks with great zeal. It achieved much in a remarkably short period and left a worthy inheritance for the new University of London.

The University Takes Over

Under the schedule to the University of London Act, a Board to Promote the Extension of University Teaching was appointed. As well as providing for the traditional work of university extension the statutes authorised BPEUT to perform a wider range of activities, including the inspection and examination of schools (other than primary, (statute 39)) and the even broader power of granting 'any certificate of proficiency in any subjects of study to any student of the University' (114).

The first meeting of BPEUT[1] took place on 5 December 1900 when the Vice-Chancellor, Professor W. A. S. Hewins, Dr C. W. Kimmins, and Sir Philip Magnus were present. At this and the remaining meetings of the session business was scrappy and attendance sparse. Things livened up a bit at the beginning of the next session though the first meeting lacked a quorum with only three members and the principal present out of a total of ten. At the following meeting on 29 October 1901 the substantial business of taking over LSEUT's affairs was discussed with attention being paid to the financial implications. It was noted that LSEUT had for many years found difficulty in obtaining funds for its work and had incurred a debt of £300 to its treasurer (Lord Hillington) which was not finally settled until 1897. Kimmins, who had been charged with producing a financial statement, referred to the sum of £150 still invested with the LCC and to the stock of syllabuses estimated to be worth £200. He expected the annual donations from public bodies, amounting to £1,150, to continue, but was more doubtful about the £200 received from private donors. In spite of his optimism that the financial question was 'by no means a serious one', financial matters again came up for discussion when BPEUT (10 December 1901) received the report of a conference between some of its members and LSEUT's representatives. This stressed the importance of help from City Livery Companies, which could only be 'maintained by direct and personal relations with them being continued'. BPEUT should have had no doubts therefore of the financial commitments of taking on the LSEUT's work.

[1]It had previously been appointed at the second meeting of the newly created Senate on 7 November 1900 and included the following members: Professor Hewins, Dr Kimmins, Dr Maclure, Sir Philip Magnus, Miss Penrose, Mr Ramsay, the Hon. W. Pember Reeves, Dr Robertson and Dr Silvanus Thompson.

To supervise the administration of BPEUT's enlarged responsibilities an exceptional person was required and members who knew about his achievements must have been confident that Roberts was the most suitable candidate for the registrarship. They therefore recommended (28 January 1902) that he should be offered the post. After some debate and a division (twenty-two in favour, three against, and two abstentions) the Senate resolved (21 March 1902) to offer Roberts the post at £500 with eight weeks' vacation. He was allowed to retain his part-time duties with the Gilchrist and Mitchell Trustees.

Once again Roberts left Cambridge to return to London and assume a range of duties that would have been overwhelming to a lesser man. As well as attending to the general conduct of BPEUT's business and its relations with the rest of the University's administration, he was charged with the supervision of two broad areas of activity: (1) University extension lectures and examinations (seventeen specific duties listed) and (2) the inspection and examination of schools (eight duties).

Under (1), the new registrar was, amongst other matters, responsible for 'the custody, multiplication of the questions at examinations, and preserving inviolate their absolute secrecy', the 'punctual preparation of syllabuses', moreover he had to 'attend meetings of Extension local committees and lectures at Extension local centres as often as may be required for the due maintenance of the efficiency of those committees' and also 'be in frequent communication with Oxford, Cambridge and Victoria University (at Manchester) for joint action in promoting the principles of the University Extension movement'.

This was only half the story as the inspection and examination of schools called for much supervision. He had, for example, 'to ascertain and certify that all conditions prescribed by the Senate had been complied with by every pupil of a school applying to be admitted to the University on the basis of a school leaving certificate (of the Board)'. Nevertheless, Roberts must have thought that he was making a good move, though the burden ultimately proved too great for he was to die a few years later (14 November 1911) at what would now be regarded the early age of sixty.[1]

[1]He had to contend with one or two acrimonious disputes with lecturers. J. Churton Collins alleged that he was not being offered sufficient lecturing appointments and wrote 'an outrageous libel on the Extension Registrar'. This was settled out of court in 1907. In extenuation of Collins' behaviour perhaps the *DNB* ought to be quoted 'long exclusion from professional posts at times embittered a kind and generous nature'.

And so the work of arranging university extension courses went on as usual – during LSEUT's last year of operations 46 sessional and 57 terminal courses were arranged and during the next year, under BPEUT's direction, there was a slight diminution (soon to be retrieved) to 37 sessional and 56 terminal courses. The cautionary note about BPEUT's finance did not pass unheeded, for every annual report continued to testify to the generosity of various public benefactors especially the City Parochial Charities, the Gilchrist, and Mitchell Trustees. There was also the first grant from the LCC in 1906 when it agreed to give £50 for each of nine sessional courses – the beginning of much needed financial help from that source.

Welcome as this assistance was there was another development – the LCC began to run its own activities leading the Lewisham centre to write to the registrar 'how can we possibly compete with the lectures run by the LCC (out of the rates) at the price of about 1s 2d the dozen with an occasional course thrown in free. There are six separate centres all easily accessible from Lewisham in these days of electric and other trains, at five of which literature courses are being run at 2s 6d for 25 lectures (1s 6d for students under 16)'. When this was discussed, at BPEUT's meeting on 27 November 1906,) Roberts pointed out that LCC lectures were intended for 'somewhat younger students' and that 'they might form excellent feeders to university extension courses if some cooperation was established'. The immediate response was for it to vote the centre £15 out of the grant from the City Parochial Charities and to instruct the registrar to communicate with the LCC about its literature lectures. Something useful must have resulted from this correspondence as the LCC voted £50 to each of ten centres wishing to promote sessional courses in history, literature and art.

The need to sustain sessional work, possibly over two or more sessions, had previously been recognised by LSEUT as a desirable objective. This policy was endorsed and expanded by BPEUT, which soon set about planning three-year (and longer) cycles of study to be given by such distinguished lecturers as Banister Fletcher, Percival Gaskell and W. H. Hudson. At a time when anthropology and sociology were in their infancy there was great interest in one of these series on the 'Evolution of Mankind as seen in the Child and the Race' in three parts, the first being given by P. Chalmers Mitchell and Professor E. A. Westermarck (1904–05) and attracting the large enrolment of over 160 students ('a really valuable piece of work suited to the requirements of teachers', according to BPEUT's report for the session).

CERTIFICATES AND DIPLOMAS

Another innovation was the award of the Chancellor's Certificate, approved in 1905, based on study and examination extending over a minimum of three sessions. That there was some dissatisfaction about this award emerged in 1908 when a memorandum was presented to BPEUT about the future of the scheme. It was estimated that the achievement of the certificate required considerable effort – 200 hours of lectures and classes, 72 essays, 1,000 hours preparing this work, together with an unspecified amount of time spent on general reading. Was it possible for suitable holders of the certificate, as at Paris, to proceed to a higher degree? Perhaps the LCC could recognise the certificate as a qualification 'for teacherships in secondary schools or head teacherships in Higher Elementary schools?' A committee was appointed to look into these matters and soon came to the conclusion that it was impossible 'by custom and statutes' to provide for higher degrees. It also expressed fears about 'diplomas in pedagogy and other professional areas', though they were happy about the idea of diplomas in the humanities. This would appear to be the origin of the establishment in 1908–09 of the diplomas in Literature, History, and Economics and Social Science.

Courses for these diplomas were restricted to the central London area and those for the fourth and final year were usually based on a School of the University. Students taking history went to University College, English literature to King's College and economics to the London School of Economics. The examination entry requirements were high especially for the fourth year, when candidates had to pass not only the subject of this final session but also those studied during the preceding three sessions. At the end of the first year of the scheme (1909–10), BPEUT reported – 'some found the strain of the work too exacting, and were unable to complete the necessary paperwork'. The slow but steady growth in the number of students taking diploma courses would seem to confirm the limited appeal of the scheme; 1909–10, 176 registered students; 1910–11, 201; 1911–12, 263; 1912–13, 338; and 1913–14, 349. When the first diplomas were awarded in 1913 there were 38 successful candidates – hardly the hundreds that LSEUT had anticipated for degree studies in its evidence to the Gresham Commission.

There was one addition to the diploma scheme before 1914 – a Diploma in the History of Art, largely due to the influence of Percival Gaskell. In his proposal for this award he reminded BPEUT how he had given courses in the history of painting, extending over six sessions, with considerable response from the 150 students enrolling for the series. Two examiners in the subject were consulted, Professors E. A. Gardner and Selwyn Image.

It was reported that 'In this country there is absolutely no degree, diploma or certificate in the subject other than the ordinary University Extension Certificate'. As Professor Gardner had further asserted that 'a diploma in the History of Art would tend to encourage a study of great importance', BPEUT readily agreed, and the Diploma in the History of Art was established in 1913 in cooperation with the Slade Committee.

NEW VENTURES

Later historians have described the Edwardian period as one of social and political unrest, indeed a book was written on 'the strange death of Liberal England' (George Dangerfield, 1935), but little of the contemporary stress seems to have been reflected in BPEUT's annual programme; courses on literary, historical and artistic subjects were the main components. These were held mainly in the inner London area with little provision in county areas where Oxford and Cambridge were still active. Occasionally a new centre would emerge, as at Ashtead, Surrey, where, during the autumn of 1909, E. M. Forster gave ten lectures on the 'Renaissance at Rome'.

Sometimes a new subject would arouse considerable interest, for example, 'Recent Researches on Bacteria' by Professor W. B. Bottomley attracted an audience of 175 at Hammersmith (autumn 1904). On the strength of this success he was nominated by BPEUT to lecture in Western Australia, supported by a grant of £100 from the Gilchrist Trustees. At the final lecture of his tour at Perth the professor was given 'an ovation such as was seldom witnessed before.' On other occasions, a lecturer, one day destined to achieve great renown, would appear in the programme. In 1908, for example, an application was received from Morley College for a course to be given by Dr Ralph Vaughan Williams on the 'Progress of Music from Haydn to Wagner'. The registrar was, however, instructed to suggest an alternative name, but, if for any reason none could be suggested, Dr Vaughan Williams was to be appointed 'if his qualifications were deemed satisfactory'. In the event Vaughan Williams gave a very successful course, enrolling over 60 students, and although he was somewhat remiss in his administrative arrangements he produced some outstanding examination results, as was noted in the examiner's report.[1]

BPEUT was always on the lookout for starting new ventures as was demonstrated by three successful summer schools, in effect the first vacation courses to be arranged on a specific subject, on 'Town Planning' at the Hampstead Garden Suburb Institute, 1912, 1913 and 1914. At this time there was a growing interest in this area, especially after the Town Planning Act (1909), and the emergence of the garden city movement. The original prospectus for the school invited men to apply and 'to use their holidays for the purpose of making themselves more familiar with the principles of town planning, the outdoor teaching being some mitigation of the sacrifice.' An impressive committee was set up to advise on the project, which owed much to the drive of the secretary of the Hampstead Garden Suburb Trust, J. S. Rathbone. It must have been a memorable experience to listen to the lecturers who included Patrick Geddes, Raymond Unwin, and A. D. Adshead, Professor of Civic Design at the University of Liverpool.

THE TUTORIAL CLASS: ORIGIN AND GROWTH

Of long lasting and momentous significance was the emergence of the tutorial class and the formation of the WEA both of which took place during the early years of BPEUT's existence. Major credit for this development is rightly ascribed to Albert Mansbridge, but less than adequate justice has been given in the histories of the movement to the contributions both of LSEUT and BPEUT.

As has been noted Toynbee Hall and especially its warden, Canon Barnett, had been greatly concerned about the provision of systematic courses for working-class students. Foreshadowing the WEA Barnett had written in 1887 'It remains now for the University Extension Society to coordinate its teaching, to give not only isolated lectures, but to guide students in the choice of courses and to provide for anyone willing to trust its care, adequate training in science, art and literature. In hospitals, the sick owe as much to

---

[1] The examiner, J. D. McClure, of Mill Hill School wrote 'This has been a really admirable course. I have had to mark some papers very strictly because of the tendency to talk about "deeper" emotions, "intensity of expression", and "subjectivity of the objective" – whatever that may mean. But in the viva voce where I got them down to facts and to the music they had heard it was clear that they had been well taught and had "the root of the matter in them".'

nursing as to the doctor's directives, and in our centres of education, the student must have not only the direction of the professor but the constant care of the tutor'. Tawney, in his contribution to Barnett's biography (by Barnett's wife, Henrietta), noted that Barnett 'desired not only greater opportunities for the higher education of working children, but also a system of University education accessible to working class men and women' and even more eloquent was his prophecy that 'the Universities might lead another Renaissance, inspire and liberate the democratic movement, humanise industry and industrial relations and be a golden link between the old world and the new'.

It was, therefore, a time for experimentation and LSEUT was persuaded by an article in the *University Extension Journal,* February 1900, on 'New Conditions and New Methods' to make a start. They agreed to support two tutorial classes at Toynbee Hall during the session 1900–01 to the extent of a £50 grant. Special conditions were laid down for these activities, clearly regarded as novel:

(1) the tutors to be appointed under the same conditions as university extension lecturers at a fee where such is necessary of £1 per class;
(2) the amount of time to be given to instruction to be equal to that usually devoted to lecture and class under ordinary conditions;
(3) a register of homework to be kept and tutors not to allow students to enter for the final examination who do not satisfy them in respect of this. As a general rule there should be six home exercises during each term;
(4) a statement of the scheme of work for the session to be sent in with applications of tutors;
(5) no definite syllabus to be required but towards the end of the session the tutor to submit an account of the ground covered, copy of which will be sent to the examiner; and
(6) the examination to be conducted as for a university extension course of instruction.

The following are the bare details of the three pioneering tutorial classes that were to break new ground, an odd mixture of tradition and innovation.

MICHAELMAS TERM
R. E. S. Hart: 'The Dissolution of the Monasteries' (part i)
H. Frank Heath: 'Tennyson' (part i)
W. R. L. Blackiston: 'Combustion and Oxidation'.

LENT TERM
R. S. E. Hart: 'The Dissolution of the Monasteries' (part ii)
H. Frank Heath: 'Tennyson' (part ii)
W. R. L. Blackiston: 'The structure of Flame'.

SUMMER TERM
R. S. E. Hart: 'The Dissolution of the Monasteries' (part iii)
H. Frank Heath: 'Tennyson' (part iii).

Hardly a programme, it might be thought, to inaugurate a new educational era! What LSEUT's council thought of the work is not reported, though they decided to renew the grant 'for the continuance of the experiment for another session'. Once again a conventional list of topics appears 'Plant Life', 'The Dissolution of the Monasteries', and 'Milton and his Achievements'.

As LSEUT was in its last session of existence there may have been a lack of drive and imagination, but perhaps this was what the students wanted, or what it was thought they should be offered. Whatever the reasons BPEUT continued along these lines, with the addition of another centre, the South Western Polytechnic, and further subjects, scarcely radical it might be thought, including 'Homer for English Readers' and 'Greek Language'.

In the meantime, the WEA had started a small branch at Battersea where Patrick Geddes gave a summer course (1907) on 'Civics' with an average attendance of 14 students. During the next session BPEUT sponsored a course under the same auspices, with Geddes again lecturing on 'Civics' during the autumn term 1907, followed by a series on the 'Outlines of the Sociology of London' by V. V. Branford. In his class report Geddes asserted that he had never had 'a course or audience (entirely skilled working class) more satisfactory than this'. He then went on 'the teaching was quite conversational, and was supplemented by visits to the British Museum and places of interest in London' – clearly a novel enterprise in BPEUT's view.

At the same time BPEUT was making, as it asserted, a 'sustained effort to bring working people into closer touch with the University Extension movement' by cooperating with 'a special organisation, the Workers' Educational Association'. The way it set about achieving this objective may now seem strange. During five successive sessions a short series of lectures, usually four meetings, were held either in Westminster, at the old University building in Burlington Gardens, or at University College.

Several thousand applications from members of trade unions, cooperative societies and other working-class organisations were received and the lectures were eventually printed and used as a publicity medium.

The first series were held on four Saturday afternoons in May 1907, at Westminster Abbey, when Professor J. H. B. Masterman lectured on the 'Story of the Abbey in relation to the History of the British People'. A large gathering of over 1,000 'working people' attended, followed by four tutorial classes limited to thirty students, which made a more detailed study of the Abbey. 'This movement among working people is full of promise, and it is likely that the coming session may see a considerable extension of the movement in the industrial districts of London' was BPEUT's prophecy. As it happened, the ever popular Masterman gave three more successive series on the 'House of Commons', 'Parliament' and the 'People and the History of London'. Noted politicians and public figures took the chair at these great gatherings, including Ramsay MacDonald, Will Crooks, and Margaret Macmillan. As far as industrial districts were concerned the main achievement was the arrangement of a short series at Woolwich on the 'History of London', by S. K. Ratcliffe, which attracted an enrolment, largely of workmen from the Arsenal, given precisely as 1,027.

Mansbridge seemed quite pleased about these ventures, especially those at Westminster Abbey where some of its great preachers, notably Canon Gore, had made such an impression earlier in his life. But the memorable conference on 'Oxford and Working Class Education' and the equally outstanding report by J. W. Headlam, HMI, and Professor L. T. Hobhouse on 'Tutorial Classes' must have inspired him to alert the Senate about the basic issues of adult education for the working classes. A letter was despatched to the University from the WEA office at 29 Buckingham Street on 16 June 1909 which read as follows: 'It is evident from numerous signs that the action of the Joint Committee on Oxford and workpeople has raised much expectation in London and consideration of the University of London has naturally arisen, it being felt that the University of London is the proper body to which workpeople should look.' It was then proposed that representatives from the University Extension Board should meet an equal number of 'representative workpeople to discuss the relationship which should exist between London workpeople and the University'.

Mansbridge, although only 33, was clearly confident, both in terms of his own abilities and his well-placed friends, of expecting a positive reply. This came when the University agreed to establish a joint committee to undertake the necessary negotiations which would lead to cooperation with BPEUT in organising 'suitable courses of instruction for artizan students'. The University representatives nominated to sit on this committee were – Dr Walmsley[1] (BPEUT's chairman), J. A. Douglas, Graham Wallas, the Principal, R. D. Roberts and those representing working people, C. W. Bowerman, MP, W. A. Appleton, Miss J. P. Madams and Albert Mansbridge. This was the origin of the Joint Committee for the Promotion of the Higher Education of Working People, destined to play such a notable rôle in the growth of the tutorial class movement in London. Archibald Ramage, compositor, and successful university extension student, and its first secretary was now entrusted with the arrangements of the first tutorial class programme under these new auspices. The arrangements for session 1909–10 were:

BATTERSEA, LAVENDER HILL COUNTY COUNCIL SCHOOL
Sociology, Patrick Geddes and J. Lionel Taylor

CLERKENWELL – WORKING MEN'S CLUB AND INSTITUTE
Economic History, F. W. Kolthammer

TOTTENHAM – FRIENDS' MEETING HOUSE
Industrial History, Henry Clay

WORKING MEN'S COLLEGE
Industrial History, Hon Gerard Collier

CROYDON ADULT SCHOOL
Social History, Gilbert Slater

There were 300 working-class applicants for the classes and, as each was limited to thirty, Ramage's task in selecting the groups could not have been easy. Successful applicants had to give a pledge to attend regularly over the three sessions envisaged for the class and submit essays. Money was readily forthcoming for the new work – £100 from the City Parochial Charities and a government grant under the Board of Education's scheme for evening classes. So successful was the first session's work that both the London and

---

[1]R. Mullineux Walmsley, (1854–1924), senior demonstrator in electrical engineering, Finsbury Technical College, 1883; later Professor of Electrical Engineering and Applied Physics, Heriot-Watt College, Edinburgh; first principal of the Northampton Institute, (1894–1924), now the City University; gave one of the earliest extension courses on the 'Electric Current' at Walthamstow, 1890; chairman of the Extension Board, (1908–22); and of Convocation, (1922–24).

Middlesex County Councils gave generous grants to enable seven additional classes to be arranged for session 1910–11. A new phase had begun in BPEUT's short history; the work steadily grew in size and was clearly regarded as a major achievement by both students and the University. To inaugurate the 1910–11 session a reception was given by the University at which the Principal, the Chairman of the Board and Roberts were present. Perhaps the most thoughtful observation on this occasion was that of one of the students. He was reported (*University Extension Bulletin,* Michaelmas 1910) as saying that 'not having had any education he had been living in a dark room which, though he had not known it, had had electric light laid on all the time. The tutorial classes had enabled him to find the switch.'

THE HALDANE COMMISSION AND THE EXTENSION BOARD

For the third time in just under twenty years the University was again the subject of an enquiry by a Royal Commission – on University Education in London – under the powerful chairmanship of R. B. Haldane. In its evidence BPEUT presented a resumé of its origins and activities, supported by the somewhat portentous statement that 'university extension serves as a sort of intelligence department whose business it is to seek to meet the needs of new classes of students and to encourage new subjects of study as well as to treat old subjects under new conditions'. Reference was also made to the diploma scheme for students unable to take degrees, 'not because they are beyond their reach, not because the standard is too high, but because the conditions that have to be fulfilled are, in the circumstances, impossible conditions'.

About the higher education of working people, BPEUT had this to say 'the tutorial side of teaching has always had a place in Extension work, although it has not always been emphasised as fully as desirable'. They stressed the importance of giving young men and women of the working classes, likely to become their leaders, 'opportunities for making a study of questions in the domain of history, economics and sociology that affect their lives – the life of the community and of coming into intimate association with university teachers who will treat disputed questions with calmness of tone and impartiality, and set an example of genuine scientific attitude and method in dealing with problems which in ordinary discussion are in danger of being confused by rhetoric, prejudice and interested partisanship'.

Having presented this temperate and elevated philosophy of adult education, BPEUT's representatives might have well anticipated a friendly reception at their examination on 21 July 1910 (present, Sir Edward Busk, chairman of Convocation, Dr Mullineux Walmsley, chairman of the University Extension Board, Dr C. W. Kimmins now chief inspector for the LCC Education Committee and Dr R. D. Roberts. Instead, attention was largely directed towards its involvement in schools examinations with little discussion about its commitment to adult education within the university.

Nearly two years later Mansbridge appeared before the commission (26 April 1912) and was greeted with great warmth and enthusiasm, as well he might have expected. One of its leading members was Sir Robert Morant, with whom Mansbridge had already had useful correspondence in his capacity as secretary to the Board of Education. Morant, in one of his letters to Mansbridge, had written about the 'very substantial work that you are getting done. We are very glad to be kept in touch here with this matter [Mansbridge's membership of the Consultative Committee of the Board of Education] and you may rest assured that we shall continue to give it our most favourable consideration.'

Even more significant was Mansbridge's friendship with Haldane, by all accounts close and cordial as he indicated in his autobiography *The Trodden Road* with his recollection of meetings in Haldane's town apartment where he was always invited to smoke a good cigar with his host. Mansbridge was therefore assured of an attentive response. After referring to the now famous *Oxford and Working Class Education,* and the thoroughness of a tutorial class 'characteristic of an honours course at Oxford', he made some radical proposals. There should be working-class representatives in the government of the University, whilst establishments such as the Working Men's College, Morley College and the polytechnics should have university recognition. Even more challenging was his proposal that students of unusual ability in tutorial classes should be given credit for that work, when embarking on a degree course, and not be expected to retrace their steps and go through the ordinary academic routine. He summed up his philosophy by asserting 'our plan is a highway of education – we do not care for the term, "ladder".'

Mansbridge, having stated his case, was then involved in a friendly dialogue with Haldane who asked 'Well, of course, a university is a body that imparts knowledge?' Back came the swift, pointed reply, 'And may I venture to say that it receives it – students (from tutorial classes) may go right beyond the university degree, dealing with first class research'. Haldane, perhaps a bit sceptical, was moved to assert, 'Well, it may be so, of course, it may be so – but that must be exceptional, must it not?' Unabashed by this gentle prodding, Mansbridge then went on to even greater heights of self-assurance, 'Not, if I may venture to say so exceptional, because a large number of students in the classes are found to do work very quickly which would be marked equal to first-class work.' Having achieved what he must have regarded as a major victory for the new movement, he paid tribute to the university's commitment – how it inspected classes, examined written work and made a careful selection of students.

As might have been expected the commission's final report (published in 1913) reflected its views of the two main types of activity of the board. After conceding that the now deceased registrar, Dr R. D. Roberts, had striven to enhance the 'thoroughness and continuity' of university extension work by establishing a diploma scheme the commission then made some critical comments 'but the conditions under which the ordinary extension courses have been given, the necessity that most of the lecturers have not been university teachers, but men who confine their teaching to giving these lectures, and that the majority of the students, though doubtless interested in intellectual things, have not been prepared to do serious work, make it impossible for a University standard to be reached in most cases'. To temper this sharp comment, unfair in some respects when one thinks of lecturers such as I. Gollancz, John Adams, G. G. Chisholm, A. F. Pollard, Graham Wallas and others of similar eminence, the commission retracted somewhat. 'A few of the students do admirable work, and the courses have undoubtedly been the means of discovery here and there of men and women who without their stimulus and assistance might have never learned to study in the University spirit. Extension lectures are also a most valuable agency for bringing large numbers of persons into touch with the University and into sympathy with its ideals. With all its limitations it is work of great value which we desire to see extended and strengthened.'

The report then continued 'there is, however, another side of the Extension work of the University which is more uniformly maintained at a high level'. There followed high praise for the recently established tutorial classes, opening up 'a new and hopeful field for the spread of a pure love of learning – the main function of a University'. Reference was also made to the enthusiasm, the zeal and the sincere desire for truth animating the students who were drawn almost entirely from the working classes. There was also a favourable comment on the lecturers 'nearly all of them men actually engaged in university teaching, and not men making their living by conducting tutorial classes'. Again a curious assertion – perhaps they disliked Collins (eventually a professor at the University of Birmingham), Banister Fletcher, W. H. Hudson, Percival Gaskell, P. H. Wicksteed and the rest who certainly did a lot of lecturing but who nevertheless regularly attracted large audiences who admired their style, method and scholarship.

Amongst the considerable amount of evidence received by the commission was a statement prepared by Goldsmiths' College staking a claim as 'a school of the University for Evening Work'. This proposition was not given much encouragement when it was asserted that evening work should be placed in a more central position and that 'the degree of success achieved by the Goldsmiths' College with its evening classes in preparation for university examinations had not been very great'.

Having come to this conclusion the commission was even less likely to act on the 'humble petition of the Mayor, Aldermen and councillors of the Metropolitan Borough of Deptford praying for the establishment in the near future of a University College for South London with low fees for evening as well as day classes.' Indeed it recommended that Goldsmiths' College with 'a building admirably suited for lectures, addresses, debates and social intercourse', should be used in the evenings, on afternoons and on Sundays, as the chief university centre for tutorial classes and that residence should be provided within its walls, if possible, for a warden who would be responsible for the organisation of its work and social life.

About the other side of BPEUT's work, the inspection of schools and schools examinations, the commission expressed definite views. They were clear in their minds that it was undesirable for the University to continue inspecting schools 'for which it cannot afford to retain the services of more than one or two full-time inspectors – it was work of a highly expert kind'. What BPEUT's inspector, Walter Rippman, thought of these sharp comments is not reported. Perhaps some consolation was derived from a letter sent by the Middlesex County Council's Education Committee to BPEUT very much regretting the proposal to end the inspections.

As regards schools examinations the commission accepted that BPEUT had a continuing role 'until the urgent national problem of school examinations is on the way to a solution'. With considerable foresight the commission expressed its conviction 'that a national system is needed and that some means must be found for bringing the various school examinations at present conducted by the different universities into line so as to ensure a general equivalence of standard without interfering with the power of the schools to adapt their curricula to local needs.'

There was one recommendation (177) however which must have caused some irritation 'we are doubtful whether the University should continue to bear the burden of supplying lectures in literary and scientific subjects or instruction in music and the fine arts for the ladies of Kensington (at King's College for Women) who can devote only their spare time to them, or as finishing courses of study for girls after leaving school, but if this is thought desirable, their organisation and supervision should be transferred to the Department for the Extension of University Teaching.'

Having expended considerable time and labour in producing a report with far-reaching conclusions, the commission saw its recommendations set aside as the gathering storms of international tension gradually led to the outbreak of the first world war. Not until the conclusion of yet another enquiry, the Hilton Young Report 1926, was there to be any further move towards reorganisation.

THE IMPACT OF THE FIRST WORLD WAR

During the period of hostilities, BPEUT, against many odds, strove to carry on its work having committed itself to the objective 'that all educational activities should be maintained in a vigorous condition not only with a view to the present needs of students, but in order that, after the war, the country might be in a position to derive full benefit from deeper national seriousness and lessened social levity, and from that fuller realisation of the responsibilities of worthy citizenship to which we may look forward'.

How far this rather extravagantly expressed objective was attained, can best be assessed by analysing the following table:

Session	Total No. of Courses	Tutorial classes and average attendance	Terminal Entries for all Courses	Average Attendance at Classes
1914–15	135	26 (544)	9,734	4,538
1915–16	114	21 (452)	6,945	3,053
1916–17	90	22 (496)	7,342	3,243
1917–18	80	21 (486)	5,470	2,855

The tutorial class programme retained an extraordinary record of consistency (compared with other types of courses). Some of its tried and experienced tutors, including Tawney, disappeared from the scene (though he was to reappear after recovering from war wounds in 1917) and other gifted tutors, Mark Hovell and A. E. Bland, were to die in action. Perhaps the most distinguished of all tutors was T. S. Eliot who conducted his literature class at Southall over three sessions 1916–18 (course fee: 2s). When he first offered his services to BPEUT his subjects, eleven in all, embraced not only various aspects of literature but also (10) sociology of primitive peoples and (11) social psychology. Although his application to give tutorial classes was approved there was apparently some doubt about adding his name to the supplementary list of university extension lecturers.

At the beginning of the war central courses, mainly in the arts, were held as usual, though in a diminishing number as its impact became more pervasive. From time to time new activities were arranged to meet changing needs – there was a considerable interest in the illustrated lectures by Allen S. Walker on architectural topics, which included buildings in London as well as the 'Cathedral Cities of Northern France and Belgium'; to these and other similar activities forces on leave were admitted free of charge. As a modest contribution towards the solution of the food problem, F. J. Crittenden gave three series of short courses on the 'Constitution and Cultivation of Soils' during 1916–17 attracting audiences of a hundred or so (at Ealing, Tottenham and the Central School of Arts and Crafts). Crittenden seems to have been a popular lecturer on horticultural topics as he was in great demand next session to give lectures on 'Garden and Food Production' at five different centres, as well as another series at Ealing on 'Food Values' and 'Some Aspects of the Growing, Harvesting and Storing of Crops'. This was followed by a course again given to his devoted audience at Ealing on 'Some Principles of Plant Cultivation in Garden and Allotment'. For two more sessions he carried on this work and then disappeared from the programme, after 1921, presumably because food supplies were now back to normal.

Towards the end of the war there was a growing interest in problems of reconstruction and both extension courses and tutorial classes reflected this concern, for example, three tutorial classes were given on this theme during 1917–18 and eight the following year. To assist BPEUT in providing extension lectures in this area £50 was forthcoming from the ever-generous Gilchrist Trustees, though there was a lengthy caveat in the letter to BPEUT about this grant (15 June 1918). In this they expressed some doubt about their decision to make the grant 'from the possibility of these lectures raising subjects of an acute controversial character and from the danger of the classroom becoming the scene of heated political discussions rather than education. They have however been influenced in their decision by the importance they attach to these studies when properly guided. They must therefore rely on the Board as well as the lecturers exercising the greatest care in these matters, and they wish that syllabuses of proposed courses should be submitted to them with applications for recognition.'

One wonders how BPEUT reacted to these magisterial requirements, with the thinly disguised anxiety that a university body might not carry out its work in the true spirit of academic impartiality. Unfortunately the perennial shortage of funds, and the unpredictability of grants and donations, meant that BPEUT could seldom be in any other situation except that of a supplicant. Yet the extra sum mentioned as being necessary for the growing demand for courses as peace approached was £5,000 – to meet 'the needs of the immense adult population of the area in which the work is conducted' – even in terms of today's purchasing power (say £50,000) this was a very modest amount.

The lecturers who eventually conducted the courses on reconstruction were, presumably acceptable, C. Delisle Burns, T. E. Gregory (later professor) and A. Milnes. Burns gave four courses, Milnes the same number and Gregory gave one; with large audiences ranging from 40 to 140.

Another novel enterprise took place during this session, the arrangement of a public lecture series in Whitehall – believed to be 'the first occasion on which a university has been invited to carry on education work in a Government office'. The audience of 350 listened to lectures by leading scholars; Graham Wallas, Professor L. W. Lyde, J. H. B. Masterman, C. Delisle Burns, Professor I. Gollancz and Professor F. C. de Sumichrast. This was followed by two short courses on historical topics in autumn 1919 and in spring 1920, attracting audiences of 310 and 146 respectively, so this must have been judged as a useful if limited enterprise.

With the signing of the armistice, some of these innovations came to an end. BPEUT was confident about the future and expressed the view, in its annual report for 1918–19, that 'University extension will be a factor of increasing importance in the further development of adult education which is by general agreement essential to the national well-being'. How far this optimism was justified and what was actually achieved is the subject of the next chapter.

Between the Wars

Towards the end of the first world war, a Committee on Adult Education was set up as part of the government's concern for post-war reconstruction. Under the chairmanship of A. L. Smith, Master of Balliol College, Oxford, it included such eloquent and forceful advocates as Albert Mansbridge and R. H. Tawney. Its task was 'to consider the provisions for, and possibilities of Adult Education (other than technical or vocational) in Britain'. Three short interim reports soon appeared on industrial and social conditions in relation to adult education, education in the Army, and libraries and museums.

The first of the three was modest in dimensions, amounting to 32 pages, and a strange mixture of lofty concern and prosaic interest in humble matters. It talked persuasively about the evil effects of monotonous labour and the need to establish works committees. In the last paragraph the writer (was it, by any chance, Tawney?) rose to great heights of rhetoric: 'The real lack in our national history has been the lack of bold and clear thinking. We have been well-meaning, we have had good principles; where we have failed is in the courage and the foresight to carry out our principles into our corporate life.'

The final report, amounting to more than 400 pages, was an impressive piece of work. As Professor R. D. Waller wrote in his foreword to its reprint under the title 'A Design for Democracy', (1956) it was 'one of the expressions of high optimism which set in at the end of the war'. Amongst its many recommendations were some important items about the universities' provision. 'We recommend' the report asserted 'that there should be established at each University a department of extra-mural education with an academic head'. There was a powerful plea for more generous financial help from national and local authorities. At a more domestic level, the CAE were keen to see closer co-ordination between the provisions for tutorial classes and university extension courses.

Yet for all its eloquence and conviction, the report appears to have made little impact on either the outlook or organisation of the University Extension Board. The only reference the UEB made in its annual report for 1918–19 was 'The provisions of the Education Act of 1918, and the recently issued Final Report of the Adult Education Committee make it clear that the extension work of the Universities is destined to hold an increasingly important place in our educational system'. Then followed a statement about its financial plight that was to be repeated almost word for word in successive reports until the final one for 1927–28. 'In very many centres the work can never be self-supporting . . . Even that part of the work that has the advantage of liberal state aid, the Tutorial Classes for Working people, cannot yet be carried on without the Board's assistance' (a reference to grants based on the surpluses that derived from fees received for inspecting and examining schools). If, as UEB finally asserted, 'the financial foundations of the work are therefore, precarious, and there is always a risk that the prospective programme in a particular year may be wrecked for want of funds', perhaps we may excuse them for being more concerned with the immediate problems of financial solvency, rather than with ambitious speculations about the future.

There were admittedly some improvements in the regulations of the Board of Education relating to grants for adult education, especially those of 1924 and 1938. But the principal beneficiaries of this assistance were tutorial classes which under skilful management usually earned 95 per cent or more of the maximum sums payable.

Although the term applied to extra-mural departments (including the University Extension Board) was 'responsible body', in many ways the rules reduced them to a state of dependency. Moreover, they were administered with little flexibility as can be illustrated by the response to a request in 1922 that a diploma course be regarded as a tutorial class for grant purposes. This was made in respect of Gilbert Slater's course at Morley College for the Diploma in Economics and Social Science. Although some financial help was given, great difficulties were encountered in a diploma course being listed under tutorial class rules which were specific about the selection and admission of students and the absence of an examination (though strangely enough the university regulations for tutorial classes did not preclude an examination if requested by the students). There the matter rested with no further application being made along these lines.

Whilst financial aid from public funds was given in some ways reminiscent of the old system of 'payment by results' (as applied to state grants to the voluntary societies providing elementary education in the nineteenth century), charitable aid was offered on a more civilised basis. This would seem to be a fair assessment of the relations between the UEB and the Gilchrist Trustees since their first grant of £100 to the former London Society in 1879. Eventually they received a letter early in 1914 in which the Trustees wrote of the considerable years over which grants had been made – but as 'educational conditions have changed so greatly, they will need to reconsider the whole question'. Nevertheless, annual grants were continued until 1921, when UEB received final notice that the Trustees were obliged, because of financial difficulties, to restrict their help to 'educational movements in their pioneer stages'. Although this was the end of a long period of generous help towards provision of class activities, the Trustees continue to have a happy relationship with the present department through the provision of generous prizes for university extension students.

As regards the organisation of extension courses the local centre played an important rôle. Some, including Bromley, Croydon, Hampstead and Watford, had existed since the days of the London Society. They were expert in arranging their programme which had to be based on a shrewd assessment of educational need and profitability. To promote a sessional class would cost a centre £98 10s 0d, or £70 if the lecturer was on the supplementary list. In return the university provided the lecturer's services, examination arrangements and certificates, the travelling library and 100 copies of the lecturer's syllabus. Travelling expenses (first class) were payable to the lecturer by the centre, if it was outside the county of London and the county borough of West Ham.

Under the Adult Education Regulations 1938, local centres could apply for a grant to supplement their revenue from fees. As this was contingent upon several specific requirements, and in any case of rather limited proportions, centres were still being advised in the handbook for 1938–39 to form themselves as University Extension Societies, with a paid-up membership (£1 1s 0d was the recommended subscription).

High Expectations but Modest Achievements

When the chairman of the Committee on Adult Education sent his report to the prime minister, he wrote in an accompanying letter 'Adult education must not be regarded as a luxury for a few exceptional persons, here and there, nor as a thing which concerns only a short span of early manhood, but an inseparable aspect of citizenship, and therefore should be both universal and lifelong . . . the opportunity should be spread uniformly and systematically over the whole community.'

How then did the University Extension Board, and its successor the University Extension and Tutorial Classes Council, fulfill these expectations during the inter-war years and what were the achievements? The answer supplied by annual statistics indicates a modest rate of growth, with tutorial classes achieving continued success.

	University Extension Courses	*Tutorial Classes*
1918–19	79	24
1923–24	118	38
1928–29	115	53
1933–34	115	59
1938–39	127	66

There was always a gap between enrolments for university extension courses and attendance at classes, reflecting the continuing emphasis on large enrolments, with students' fees playing a large part in the finances of this work (e.g. 1933–34, 7,767 terminal entries to courses, with 4,491 attendances at classes).

The concentration of a large proportion of the UEB's (and later the UETC's) work in the LCC's area is noteworthy, for example, in 1925 out of a total of 160 courses, 128 were held in this area, and in 1938, 149 out of 193. The failure to carry the work further afield was due to a variety of causes. Apart from the long established centres, local effort was often unpredictable, a situation that persisted in the provision of tutorial classes until the appointment of the first resident organising tutor in 1937 (L. G. Stone). There was also the problem of transport and although the train service was probably as good as, if not better than, today's provision, private motoring was in its infancy. This must have restricted the development of activities in places not easily approached by public transport. However, roots were occasionally laid down in new centres; for example, R. F. Harrod gave two tutorial classes at Woking between 1924–26. Another successful and popular tutor, Margaret Cole, travelled to Dartford, also for two sessions 1925–27, to deliver her class on English social and industrial history. There appears however to have been trouble because the class met in the local Labour

Party Office. This was the subject of a letter from the Board of Education in which it was stated 'In general the Board do not consider it desirable that classes should be conducted in premises which are identified with a particular political organisation'. The class secretary wrote about his difficulties – 'the high charges for and the inconvenient situation of two other rooms offered' stating that other agencies as well as the Labour Party used the accommodation. A suitable reply was despatched to the Board of Education and the joint committee resolved, in a rather non-committal way, that 'the organising secretary should at his discretion advise prospective students as to the suitability or otherwise of their proposed meeting place'.

MAINTAINING THE EXTENSION PROGRAMME

University extension activities during the wars were based on two main objectives – the provision of 'systematic and continuous teaching', based mainly on diploma courses, and the creation of a general interest in various liberal subjects. Diploma courses, especially those shortened to two sessions, attracted a distinctive audience. The most popular was the Diploma in Literature with some 200 students achieving the award (mainly at King's College) between the wars.

One innovation, the Diploma for Civic Workers, had a brief and unpropitious existence. Arrangements for this award designed as part of the Diploma in Economics and Social Science (such was the flexibility of administrative procedures) were announced in 1919. It was launched with the blessing of the boards of studies in Hygiene and Public Health, and Sociology and covered two broad topics – 'conditions of social and industrial well-being' and 'conditions of health'. It would appear to have been designed for what are now styled social workers and this may explain why William Temple, (then Canon of Westminster), chairman of the Board to Promote Religious Training for Social Workers, sent a note to the University Extension Board. In this he referred to the omission in the syllabus of theology and Christian ethics. Thereupon the study of Christian ethics and the principles of social life was included as an optional subject. Various courses at Bedford College, King's College for Women and the London School of Economics were approved for the diploma. There seems, however, to have been a great dearth of students, ascribed to shortcomings in publicity. At a meeting of the UEB it was suggested, rather extravagantly, that further courses might be launched at 'the Borough Polytechnic as well as in Hampstead, Highgate, Lewisham, Wandsworth, Woolwich, etc'. Nothing came of these expansive ideas and all that appears in the board's reports is the solitary achievement of one student who obtained the diploma in 1923.

A more productive enterprise was that proposed and launched by the Church of England Temperance Society, again based on the Diploma in Economics and Social Science. Early in 1926 the Temperance Society applied for recognition as a centre to provide a diploma course to meet the needs of prospective police court missionaries (probation officers) at a time when the Home Office was paying attention to their educational standards. After some correspondence with the Joint Universities' Council for Social Studies and the Magistrates' Association, the proposal was accepted with the requirement that the training should be 'free from political or other bias'. It was to be a mixture of theoretical study and practical work, the latter arranged by the Temperance Society in consultation with UEB. The syllabus, largely the work of Gilbert Slater, was an interesting and novel adaptation of the diploma scheme and included the study of 'the causes of poverty e.g. defects in national, industrial and commercial organisation, unemployment, underemployment, blind-alley occupations, drink, improvidence, preventible disease and remedial measures, and agencies, voluntary and government'. Slater was employed to give three courses between 1926 and 1929; to be followed by a fourth course, somewhat original at the time, on the psychology of crime and criminal law and administration. One of the students on the course was R. A. Pestell (now the Lord Wells-Pestell). At that time he was keen to take up a career in social work and was advised to study for the diploma as there were very few alternative opportunities for training. 'It was a demanding course', he writes, 'well organised and gave me an excellent grounding for my future work in the probation service.'

Diploma courses were arranged from 1935 in LCC institutes and a series for the Diploma in Economics and Social Science was held between 1935 and 1939 at the Eltham Literary Institute. Three of the courses were given by Hugh Gaitskell, 'Modern Economic System', 'Economic & Monetary Theory', and 'Studies in Public Finance'; and the fourth on 'English Economic History' by Ivy Pinchbeck. This must have been a remarkable experience for the faithful band of students who attended the lectures given by a future Chancellor of the Exchequer. One of them was Mrs Audrey Callaghan (wife of the present Prime Minister). She recalls with special affection Hugh Gaitskell's lectures, 'he was', she writes, 'a dedicated teacher, and we worked hard together under his guiding influence. Discussions were keen and full of thrust as this was the time when Keynes' writings especially his *General Theory on Employment, Interest and Money* (1936) were commanding great attention. We had to write weekly essays and the standards of the examinations were high. After the meetings, two or three students were given a lift on our way home, yet another indication of Hugh's kindness. I have always regarded this grounding in economics an important factor in my public life'.

By 1938 there were five diplomas: History, Literature, Economics and Social Science (about to be divided into two separate schemes), History of Art, and the Literary, Historical and Comparative Study of the Bible. During the session 1938–39 of the total of 440 students registered for the diplomas, 114 were studying literature and 221 economics and social studies. The regulations required considerable enterprise on the part of the diploma students, they were required to attend at least three-quarters of the total number of meetings and to write 16 essays each session. Examinations (as now) were held at the end of each session, but unless the candidate obtained a merit mark in each of the first three sessions he had to take an interim examination on the previous three years' work. Failure to achieve a pass of merit standard meant that he was not allowed to take his fourth-year course and the final examination. These regulations may in some measure have been responsible for the small number of students ultimately achieving their diploma, for example, at the end of the session 1938–39 these amounted to History, 12; Literature, 28; Economics, 23; History of Art, 2; and Study of the Bible, 6.

A successful candidate, therefore, might reasonably well expect some reward for his labour, though there was less concern about equivalence with other awards, especially degrees, than has been the experience recently. He was presented with his diploma by the Chancellor at the annual presentation in May (the last being 1939) and furthermore was given a complimentary ticket entitling him to admission to all central courses for two sessions.

The rest of the extension programme displayed a mixture of innovation and conservatism. Sometimes a new subject would generate, if only for a short period, considerable demand. For example, Cyril Burt gave two short courses on 'the measurement of intelligence by the Binet-Simon tests' and Professor John Adams a similar series during the session 1919–20, for these the audiences ranged from one to three hundred students.

At this time wireless telephony, as it was then called, was beginning to make its impact and it would be intriguing to know what F. Womack, MB, BSc, discussed in his short courses of three lectures on this subject during the session 1922–23. And, how did he acquire the necessary expertise? (his first lectures were in 1895 on 'The Earth and its Luminaries'). Still he attracted an audience of 128 at Hatch End, 150 at Hounslow and 95 at South Tottenham – a rare example of an extension course holding its own against the newly established technical colleges.

Within the inner London area the traditional centres, including Gresham College, the Victoria and Albert Museum, Morley College and the Saint Bride Foundation, continued to provide the main centres for extension courses, with average audiences of fifty students or more. Occasionally a new partnership was formed to the advantage of both sides, for example, that involving the London Cooperative Societies' Joint Education Committee from 1932. By the session 1938–39 this had led to the provision of four sessional courses; at Croydon (lecturer, E. C. Fairchild), Greenwich (H. L. Beales), Enfield Highway (C. A. Smith) and at Toynbee Hall (G. Darling). Out of the Divinity Lecturers' Committee, set up in 1924, there later emerged, in 1932, the Association for Adult Religious Education. Under the inspiration of Miss Marjory West, a distinguished lecturer in this field, the association arranged several successful courses (held at University College) for the Diploma in the Study of the Bible.

Between the wars twenty courses were organised, in co-operation with the Central Association for Mental Welfare, for school medical officers making a special contribution to the problems, as it was then called, of mental deficiency. In 1946 the partnership was resumed with the newly styled National Association for Mental Health. Under the guiding influence of Ronald Knowles, these courses, dealing with mentally subnormal children, achieved national fame – the last was held in 1970.

During the last years of the thirties there was talk about the need for a national revival of the university extension movement, as some prophets had spoken of its imminent decline. What then was the situation in London during the session 1938–39? The programme consisted of; 47 sessional, 47 terminal and 33 short courses, and represented 38 per cent of extension activities for the whole country – no small achievement. As well as the traditional pattern of diploma and other sessional courses a wide diversity of topics was covered in the shorter series, for example, Sir Bernard Pares gave his ten-lecture course at Marylebone and Woking on 'England and World Politics' and an abbreviated version of six lectures at Hampstead, whilst a series on the 'World Outlook' attracted an audience of some 900.

Much of the work was undertaken by veteran lecturers Sir Banister Fletcher, Sir John Marriott and Percival Gaskell. There was also the indefatigable Allen S. Walker whose encyclopaedic knowledge of London (derived not from an academic career, but from his early work as research assistant to Sir Walter Besant, historian of London) enabled him, also during this last pre-war session, to give 18 short courses totalling 90 lectures on a wide variety of architectural themes. His first course, a tutorial group based on Canon Masterman's lectures on Westminster Abbey, had been given in the summer of 1907 and his final lecturing took place during 1939–40.

Perhaps the movement had become set in its ways, and had lost something of its original impetus. Undoubtedly financial pressures severely limited expansion and the immediate prospects, somewhat gloomy, received a further blow with the outbreak of the second world war.

Tutorial Classes Gather Momentum

An important event in the history of the tutorial class movement in London was the appointment of G. D. H. Cole as staff tutor from 1922 to 1925; he then left to become Reader in Economics at Oxford. The initial impetus to this development was a memorandum from H. P. Smith (secretary, since 1919, of the London District of the WEA) on the Status and Tenure of Tutors. It was submitted to the Joint Committee for the Promotion of Higher Education of Working People, of which Smith was joint honorary secretary.

The main contention was that one or more full-time tutors should be appointed with the status of internal teacher, in order to maintain high standards of work within the movement. This was readily accepted and a small committee, comprising Sir Gregory Foster, Sir William Beveridge, John Lea, J. M. Mactavish, Miss J. P. Madams and H. P. Smith, was appointed to frame conditions of employment. It was decided that the annual salary should be £500, and that the tutor should take four tutorial classes and give additional tuition when required. There was also the general requirement that he was to do such things as might preserve and develop the movement, to bring the work to the notice of undergraduates, and encourage cooperation between part-time tutors. At its meeting early in 1922, the joint committee discussed the suitability of existing tutors for the post, and enquiries were despatched to possible candidates – to Mrs S. S. Brierley, Messrs Cole, Piercy and Tawney. Another tutor, W. H. Pringle, then in New Zealand, was sent a cable inviting his application.

The results of these negotiations are interesting. Piercy declined, and Tawney prevaricated, leaving Cole and Mrs Brierley in the field. In the meantime, Pringle despatched a brief telegram – 'Yes, if no objections outside work bringing £200'. Eventually Mrs Brierley, Cole and Pringle were summoned for interview – the last having been advised that his condition of outside earnings of £200 was not acceptable, though other remunerative work such as writing books or articles would be permitted.

In her biography *The Life of G. D. H. Cole,* Dame Margaret Cole offers an additional insight into this episode derived from a letter written by H. P. Smith. According to this account, two candidates were invited for interview, but the committee was split down the middle, the Labour side (all but one) preferring the safe candidate (presumably Pringle), and the University members (again with one exception) voting for Cole. In the end, so the account runs, Sir Gregory Foster (chairman) gave his casting vote to Cole.

Something of a mystery attaches to the other candidate, Mrs Brierley, who presumably was not summoned to the interview. At that time she was taking four classes in psychology – a third year at Morley College, a second year at Croydon, and first-year classes at St Pancras and Wandsworth. They all seemed to be going well though there had been several absences due to illness at Wandsworth. Why then was it resolved at the end of the session 'that the organising secretary be instructed not to arrange any new classes for Mrs Brierley next session'? Beyond this short statement, the minutes are silent, but further light can now be shed on the episode. In her biography Margaret Cole wrote, that her husband 'fought and won a battle with his employers when they proposed to terminate the services of a married woman tutor who had gone off with a member of one of her classes; this defence of the Permissive Society in the world of adult education made a considerable stir at the time'. Research indicates that the teacher in question was Mrs S. Brierley, later Susan Isaacs, and that she resumed and continued teaching in tutorial classes until 1933. As well as a pioneer in the field of child psychology she was a gifted teacher of psychology to adults, proving that it was possible 'to present this difficult subject intelligibly and attractively to non-technical audiences and without losing scientific soundness'.[1]

Fortunately for the movement, Cole was no newcomer to adult education. His first introduction was in 1913, when, in his early twenties, he gave six lectures on 'Rousseau' at the Oxford Summer School. Then during session 1916–17 he conducted his first tutorial class. This was on 'Reconstruction after the War' and was held at Holborn Hall, Clerkenwell, with a group which included a number of 'restive and argumentative young Guild Socialists'. As well as bringing valuable experience to his new post, he introduced new ideas which were to bear fruit not only during his short term of office but in the succeeding years. One of his classes took the form of a rôle-playing exercise, based on the model of a joint council for the railways, whilst another used the methods of a social survey to study 'The King's Road and its Neighbourhood'.

The advanced tutorial class was very much Cole's creation. One such class which he gave during session 1925–26 was based on a study of the 'British Working Classes, 1846–70', with Cole attending on alternate weeks, leaving the group to discuss each other's papers, which ultimately formed chapters in one of his books. 'I am convinced' he wrote in his report 'that this kind of class is excellently adapted for advanced work. The fact that I attend fortnightly instead of weekly is a positive advantage since it throws more on the students and gives them confidence.'

When the group eventually disbanded at the end of the following session, Cole reported that several members were already taking classes for the WEA. This was a method of recruiting tutors to which he paid special attention by setting up training groups for third-year students. He enlarged on this idea at the Coming-of-Age Convention of the WEA in 1924, when he stressed the need to encourage 'our own students to undertake teaching work . . . We have at present too few tutors drawn from the ranks of students and too much of the university atmosphere in our own work. I value the university connection as a means of maintaining standards of work, but we must not allow it to overshadow us or to obscure the essential character of our problem and our organisation.'

[1]Obituary note, *The Times*, 3 October 1948, Susan S. Isaacs, CBE, 1885–1948, was largely responsible for the growth of the Department of Child Development at the Institute of Education where she was head, 1933–43. She was also psychologist at the London Clinic of Psycho-Analysis; and played a leading part in the British Psychological Society.

Although the duties of staff tutor (then as now) were exacting, involving a good deal of travelling and evening work, Cole retained much energy for other activities. At this period he was largely responsible for the growth of the Tutors' Association, and for the invaluable *Tutor's Handbook* (1923). His wife, Margaret, took her first classes at Croydon and Dartford in 1925–26, and has written evocatively on those days. 'I have lectured to the accompaniment of a shunting-yard, a choral class conducted by a distinguished modern musician, and *underneath* the meeting-place of a remarkable religious sect, which registered inspiration by collectively jumping up and down on the floor; one of Douglas's classes was held in a building in which it was sandwiched between a company rehearsing Gilbert and Sullivan and a bunch of Army recruits learning to play the drums.' Students and tutors since then could, no doubt, recount equally lively evenings and would likewise support Dame Margaret Cole's final view of an adult class 'It is a great satisfaction when you pull it off, but a miserable evening when you fail.'

Fortunately for his students Douglas Cole was to continue taking classes until session 1930–31, whilst Margaret maintained an even longer contact. She taught until the 1940s when she gave classes at Morley College on 'Economics in the Modern World' (1942–43), and on 'Post-War Reconstruction', with O. Gollancz, (1943–44).

Another tutor who has written warmly about his experiences during what must have been exciting years was Dr Charles Hill (later Lord Hill of Luton). In his autobiography, *Both Sides of the Hill,* he recalls his classes in biology at Hampstead, and then at Morley College where he taught for three successive years, 1927–30. As a young medical student he readily took up part-time teaching to supplement his scanty income from grants, two years before and three years after qualifying. 'The world of adult education' he relates 'was quite new to me. I was a young man of twenty-one, who had shown no outstanding enthusiasm for education, and here were middle-aged men and women, voluntarily attending weekly classes in serious subjects, not because they wanted to earn more or get a degree or a diploma, but because they genuinely wanted to enlarge their minds.' He obviously enjoyed the work, especially at Morley College, where he encountered, amongst others: C. E. M. Joad, 'whose philosophy classes were always oversubscribed'; Eva Hubback, then the college's principal, 'a distinguished campaigner for minority causes', and Barbara Wootton (by this time, Director of Studies for Tutorial Classes), 'one of the ablest women of her generation.

I knew enough of her academic triumphs to be slightly scared of her', he writes. Dr Hill's reports on his classes make interesting reading. 'The work of this class [second year in biology at Morley College, 1929–30] has been extremely satisfactory. During most of the term, the second hour has been devoted to the practical dissection of vertebrate animals. Frogs, dogfish, guinea pigs and rabbits have been studied at the dissection board. Some excellent dissected specimens were exhibited at the annual Open Day at Morley College. An initial timidity mastered, the students quickly realised the abiding nature of knowledge acquired first hand.' At a time when Dr Hill's classes were the only two (out of a total of 54) on scientific topics, this was clearly an outstanding performance.

COLE AND HIS IMPACT ON TUTORIAL CLASSES

Shortly after leaving London for his new post at Oxford, Cole put down his thoughts on the organisation of the WEA and tutorial classes in the London district in a memorandum (January 1927) addressed to the chairman of the Joint Committee. It was clearly judged to be an important statement and was sent to all members of the committee for their consideration.

In many ways, the analysis is as relevant today as it was fifty years ago. Cole noted the problems of organisation in the London area: first, its size and complexity made it difficult to create areas based on 'a strong local life'. Then, there was the LCC's education policy, which as well as having good points, created some difficulties – charges for premises used for tutorial classes were too high, and co-ordination between this work and evening institutes was not always easy. The relationship between tutorial classes and the WEA was the subject of comment. Cole advocated a clear division of labour. The Joint Committee should assume responsibility for all types of grant-earning classes, including terminal and sessional, leaving the WEA the task of organising the programme for which a grant would be payable.

Critical attention was directed towards the Joint Committee – 'not a satisfactory body, partly because of its personnel, and partly because of its methods of work'. What was meant by this statement is not immediately apparent – perhaps it was intended to suggest that difficulty was caused by the division of the committee into two groups, one nominated by the Board to Promote the Extension of University Teaching,[1] and the other by the WEA[2]. In addition, the requirement of reporting to UEB, and not direct to the Senate, was regarded as a source of irritation.

It was clear in Cole's mind that the appointment of 'a fit academic head' to co-ordinate the work was a crucial requirement. The title proposed was Director of Studies, and he recommended that a staff tutor be appointed. As there had only been one so far, Cole himself, it is possible that he envisaged himself as the first holder of the post.

Cole asked important questions about the teaching staff. Were staff tutors most effectively employed in taking four classes, or should they more properly be assigned to pioneering work, including short courses in new areas? The latter was clearly Cole's view, though he failed to provide an answer to the perennial problem – what would happen when a successful class established by an experienced tutor was taken over by one who was less effective?

There followed some sharp comments on the part-time tutor with Cole asserting that there were far too many casual appointments of persons unlikely to take much interest in the movement outside the classroom. The logic of this view was that the most satisfactory part-time tutors should give a large number of classes, assisted by suitable students, who might be trained for the work. He was also keen to relieve the Joint Committee of responsibility for appointing tutors, by empowering the organising secretary, the director of studies and chairman, to approve names. Before coming to the main proposal in the memorandum, the appointment of a director of studies, it has to be noted that there was only one reference to the other half of the University Extension Board's work and that not particularly flattering. 'It is clearly absurd for one-year classes (tutorial) to be regarded as unsuitable for university control when extension courses certainly of no more advanced character are accepted without demur.' Perhaps this symbolised the bifurcation of the work, embracing differing philosophies, and

[1]Dr E. Barker (later Sir Ernest), Sir William Beveridge, Dr C. W. Kimmins, John Lea (University Extension Registrar), Dr G. Senter, Miss E. Strudwick, and Professor Dover Wilson.
[2]C. Brandon, T. W. Burden (London District, WEA), Miss J. P. Madams, Co-operative Union, G. Parkhurst, L. G. Stone, H. S. Toynbee and Barbara Wootton (also London District, WEA).

leading to divisions which increasingly became entrenched as the years went by.

BARBARA WOOTTON AS DIRECTOR OF STUDIES

When Cole's document was eventually discussed at the Joint Committee's meeting on 12 May 1927 a resolution was passed that 'the Senate be recommended to empower the University Extension Board to appoint, on the recommendation of the Joint Committee a Director of Studies'. Terms of appointment were drawn up: the director was to act as head of the tutors, and be responsible for their efficient conduct. He was to report on syllabuses, advise on all tutorial matters, take two classes, and generally to do all in his power to promote and advance the development of the movement. Then followed the specific recommendation that the post be offered to Barbara Wootton.

When news of this proposal reached the ears of the London Group of the Association of Tutorial Class Tutors there was a lively reaction. This was communicated in a letter sent by Margaret Cole (its honorary secretary) to the Joint Committee. Whilst they were not in any way astonished or disappointed about the annual salary (£600), they were amazed at the failure to advertise the post as widely as possible. Back came an official reply from A. T. Mitcheson in which he asserted that the Joint Committee would be equally as astonished as the tutors' group because their recomendation had not yet been adopted by the Senate.

Perhaps the tutors were a little precipitate, though not without reason, if they thought that widest publicity should have been given to the new appointment. All came out well in the end when Barbara Wootton eventually took up the new post in September 1927. She herself had some misgivings at first because she had been principal of Morley College for less than two years. Still, £600 a year, notwithstanding the tutors' concern, and the absence of a marriage bar, helped to persuade her to accept.

For the next seventeen years Barbara Wootton carried out her duties with exemplary efficiency, adding even greater renown to the provision of tutorial classes in the London area. There was, as she explains in her autobiography, *In a World I Never Made,* a kind of dyarchy in the Joint Committee's work. Her responsibilities were academic, whilst the organising secretary (first John Davidson, then P. R. Higginson) attended to administra-

tive matters. The supervision of classes (as colleagues in the present department will know) involved a considerable amount of travel, and an equally
detailed knowledge of the geography of the metropolis. Moreover she
'formed strong views as to the relative efficiency of the street lighting systems
provided by the various Borough Councils; for many of the meeting places
were tucked away in clubs, or church halls, or very occasionally public
houses in obscure back streets and very difficult to find.'

In spite of all these difficulties and others, she mentions, for example, the
problem of reconciling the popularity of lectures with high educational
standards, Barbara Wootton found her work a rewarding experience. She
greatly enjoyed and profited from her various classes, a view warmly
reciprocated by many of her students who, years later, still recall not only
her outstanding teaching, but also her frequent private acts of kindness.
Regarding the wider impact of extra-mural teaching on the academic
profession, which she thought 'a valuable experience for any university,
teacher', her observations have a continuing relevance. 'In these classes'
she wrote 'one does not enjoy the luxury of a captive, or even a semi-
captive, audience. If your extra-mural lectures are boring or do not give the
students what they want, the class vanishes and so does your fee. The extra-
mural teacher has, therefore, a strong inducement to pay attention to his
security as a teacher as well as to his competence in his subject. Inside the
walls of the university, on the other hand, a snobbish indifference to pedago-
gic skill has long prevailed and has not yet been overcome.'

Besides Cole and Barbara Wootton, there were other full-time staff who
gave the movement distinguished service at this time. Cole's successor was
R. S. Lambert, chosen, in preference to C. E. M. Joad, out of six part-time
tutors who were invited to apply for the vacancy. Joad, then 33, gave as his
reason for applying, a wish to leave the Civil Service (Ministry of Labour)
and to devote all his time to the tutorial class movement. He offered to
teach literature, philosophy, political theory and psychology, but he admitted
that he had no experience in the last subject. Although unsuccessful, Joad
continued to take both tutorial and extension classes, and achieved great
popularity amongst adult students, as he did later at Birkbeck College.
Lambert's employment was brief for he resigned in April 1927 to take an
important post in the Adult Education Department of the BBC.

A second staff tutorship was authorised by the Board of Education in 1925,
and in September D. A. Ross was appointed out of 105 applicants. Mrs

Cole refers to him as 'the most original and wayward of my friends' and further asserted that he was 'more personally unaccountable, honest, disconcerting and entertaining than most people put together'. He died unhappily at the early age of 40 in a motor accident, though he had left the University by that time. The other full-time staff were W. E. Williams, Miss G. M. Colman and W. L. Kendall, and special mention must be made of L. G. Stone, the first resident staff tutor (a former student) appointed to work in south east Essex in 1937.

Most of the work had necessarily to be undertaken by part-time staff, who, as well as having high academic qualifications, were especially chosen for their understanding of the needs and outlook of working-class students. Some were Cole's friends, for example, E. F. M. Durbin, Hugh Gaitskell and Michael Stewart; others were university teachers, writers and public figures who achieved fame in their different callings. Names that figured in the annual programmes included H. L. Beales, J. M. Blackburn, H. J. Boyden, H. W. Durant, F. J. Fisher, D. W. Harding, Kingsley Martin, Krishna Menon and Stephen Potter.

Unfortunately less is known about the students, though several later achieved adult scholarships and studied successfully at the University, especially at the London School of Economics. They were required to give the substantial pledge to attend weekly over three consecutive sessions and to write essays on subjects set periodically by the tutor. The fees charged were (compared with those in extension courses) low, generally 5s for the session, and courses were held throughout the London area, with a certain amount of concentration at successful centres, including Morley College, Toynbee Hall and Harrow.

Tutors' reports on their classes make interesting reading; they invariably refer to the keenness of the students and their devotion – though there were the occasional disappointments. In an account of his class at Morley College, 1926–27, Kingsley Martin reported that three students left 'because the tutor was not a Marxist'. Stephen Potter was a popular literature tutor, and during 1937–38 took a second-year class on the 'History of English Literature' attended by civil servants at the Ministry of Labour, Ruskin Avenue, Kew. It met at the agreeable hour of 4.30 pm, and the tutor wrote: 'The continued and especial keenness of this class seems to show that civil servants employed (as they usually are) in work which fails to satisfy the rather high mental ability through which they got their jobs, make admirable recruits for the WEA.' By this time white-collar workers were clearly welcome in tutorial classes (in sharp contrast to an incident in 1913 when a class at Bromley was severely criticised for having too high a proportion of teachers). Nevertheless, the emphasis remained on the needs of 'wage-earning people who are unable to pursue courses of study within the University' and there was a rule that 'university graduates and other persons not covered by the term "working men and women" should be admitted to Tutorial Classes in exceptional circumstances only'.

For all the drive of the University, the WEA, and other interested parties, the movement, despite its high renown, catered for a small number of the adult population. During the session 1938–39, sixty-six tutorial classes recruited 1,156 students, of whom 418 were in first-year classes. The same was also true for students registered for diplomas in the humanities (440). The question must be asked, though it is more difficult to answer, why was the interest of such small proportions; were the requirements for class membership too rigorous; did the harsh realities of unemployment create difficulties; or was the general approach of the classes too conventional? There could be something in this last possibility. About this time another movement, the Left Book Club, which asked its members to become serious students as well as active members, succeeded in recruiting very widely.

SUMMER SCHOOLS FOR TUTORIAL CLASS STUDENTS

By the beginning of the century the residential summer meeting was a well-established institution at Oxford and Cambridge. Although it was a popular event, there was the occasional critic, for example, Charles Wibley. In his carping article, published in the *Nineteenth Century,* 1894, entitled 'The Farce of University Extension', there appeared the following onslaught: 'For three weeks at a time, the Universities are invaded by a mob of intellectual debauchees, whose ambition is far greater than their stomach, and who sit them down to an orgy of information which is warranted to leave the stoutest with a mental dyspepsia.' Whether Wibley ever attended a summer meeting is not recorded, but if by chance he had visited the first WEA summer school at Oxford in 1910, he would probably have formed a different opinion. For eight weeks a gathering of studious manual workers came under the influence of a team of dedicated tutors, the result of A. L. Smith's view that 'men should come from tutorial classes to Oxford, bringing their special difficulties and requests for further information, to be dealt with by tutors working in an individual way'.

Albert Mansbridge, with his considerable knowledge of these Oxford summer schools, was no doubt responsible for the Joint Committee's decision to explore the possibility of holding its own school in 1914. Enquiries were made about suitable locations and the proposal for a residential school at Isleworth was discussed in committee, whilst some class secretaries, on being asked to express an opinion, suggested a seaside resort. Mansbridge, no doubt, thought of a more impressive venue, to match the spires and cloisters of his favourite Oxford, and he may well have suggested Eton College. This idea was readily accepted, and an enquiry was despatched to the provost and fellows. They agreed to house the proposed summer school, but had to regret that 'chiefly owing to the necessity of carrying out cleaning and repairs during the holidays, the boys' rooms would not be available'. Rooms for tuition and the office could be provided in the college as well as 'space for a camp'. Then came the welcome response to the Joint Committee's appeal for financial help – they would make a grant of ten shillings a student towards the costs of lodgings or a camp, up to a maximum sum of £50.

This was a very acceptable offer, especially at a time when the Joint Committee were looking around for extra resources to further their work. Early in 1914 an attractively printed report of the work during the first four years of its existence was published. Because their appeal for funds is an interesting commentary on current ideas and philanthropy, some details are presented.

The achievements were set out in tables and further emphasised by reference to tutors' reports – 'they may not have become better wage-earners, but I believe they have all become better citizens', was a typical comment.

In particular there were four immediate financial needs: to avoid the present annual deficit (then running at £613); to pay the tutors an adequate remuneration; to provide a really efficient travelling library; and to provide funds for arranging advanced courses of lectures (the average cost of a class was given as £81 2s 10d).

The sum specified for advancing the work was £500 rising to £1,000 over three successive years, and the report (with an enclosed banker's order form) was given an extensive circulation to certain 'influential and wealthy persons likely to respond to the appeal'. The list of persons is a fascinating document composed by a expert on charitable appeals – descending the social ladder it gave the names of the following: five dukes, two marquesses, ten earls, nine viscounts, twenty-eight lords, twenty-five privy councillors, thirty-seven baronets, sixteen knights and seventy-eight MPS. The intriguing list of miscellaneous persons included, amongst others, Mrs Bernard Shaw (but not Shaw himself), Andrew Carnegie and the governors of the London School of Economics. Committee members were, in addition, invited to specify 'employers of labour with works in London, members of the Stock Exchange, Bishops, educational trusts and city companies'. Yet, for all this endeavour, only £10 10s was received and this was a donation from Lord Claud Hamilton. There was little else the Joint Committee could do when it met to discuss the appeal and its response, except to thank Lord Claud Hamilton.

With this miserable experience very much in their minds, the Joint Committee must have been rather anxious about the forthcoming experiment at Eton, especially as enrolments looked like being small. Undaunted by the likelihood of a rebuff, the chairman (Sir Henry Miers, who was, after all, principal of the University) wrote to the provost and fellows inviting them to revise the conditions of their financial help and to pay a fixed sum in place of the capitation grant of 10s a student. Always generous, they substituted an unconditional grant of £35, together with £5 for needy students.

Eventually twenty-two students took up their different residences around Eton College from 1–15 August 1914, the first, if not poor, certainly working-class, scholars to be attached to the leading boys' public school. It was regarded as a disappointing response. The reasons given were lateness of publicity and competing schools, held at Oxford, Cambridge, Bangor and Durham, regarded more attractive than Eton. Nevertheless the school was judged a great success, educationally and socially. The programme was intensive, with daily lectures and discussions, as well as private tuition which averaged five hours a week. The topics were mainly related to history, literature and philosophy, the only lecture that appeared to relate to the imminent outbreak of war was that given by A. E. Zimmern on 'The Present Situation'.

What did it mean to the students, who included six engineers, five clerks, two tailors, two joiners, a fishmonger, needlewomen and other manual workers? No doubt they were impressed by the generous hospitality; there were talks about Eton, visits, an organ recital and entertainment for the 'ladies of the party'. One student wrote that everything proceeded 'as merry as a marriage bell', whilst the tutors made equally complimentary remarks. A. E. Bland, for example, asserted that it had been 'a supremely happy and fruitful time'. The final balance sheet must have been regarded as very satisfactory, though it involved a small deficit of £2 7s 8d.

Grants	Income			Expenditure			
	£	s	d		£	s	d
Eton College	35	0	0	Tutors' fees	45	0	0
Other sources	5	5	0	Food	45	2	0
Board of Education	50	0	0	Lodging	13	11	6
Students' fees	22	2	0	Two scholarships	2	10	0
				Printing	5	4	8
				Miscellaneous	3	6	6
*Balance	2	7	8				
	£114	14	8		£114	14	8

*Presumably covered by University funds.

It was just over a decade before the next summer school was held from 18 July to 1 August 1925 in the far different surroundings of Easton Lodge, near Dunmow, Essex. Nothing now remains of this once famous country seat of Frances Evelyn, Countess of Warwick. At the time of her marriage she was the richest heiress in the country and a well-known society lady. When she eventually joined the Social Democratic Federation in 1905, her views, behaviour and entourage underwent a considerable change. Thereafter, she became one of the most controversial and influential protagonists of advanced socialist ideas in Britain.

Sometime during the first world war she must have met G. D. H. Cole. Writing in his diary in May 1919, S. L. Bensusan, her close confidant, noted that 'Lady W has a great belief in revolution and G. D. H. Cole'. When the Joint Committee resumed its discussions about a summer school, early in 1925, Cole had already thought of Easton Lodge as a likely venue. By this time it had already achieved fame as a desirable location for such ventures, especially in radical circles.

It was magnificently situated and approached by a two-mile drive through twelve hundred acres of parkland. The house still reflected the pomp and splendour of Edwardian times (as well as some of its discomforts) and Lady Warwick was well renowned for her generous hospitality.

How far the Joint Committee approved of this establishment is hard to say. In the minutes of its meeting held on 22 January 1925, there is a cryptic reference to Cole's negotiations: 'It was not known to what extent the staff tutor, acting under the authority of Sir Gregory Foster, the late chairman, had committed the Joint Committee. After some discussion, it was decided that the scheme had to be carried through if the committee were too deeply involved to withdraw, but if this was not the case, further action to be left to the Chairman, who if not satisfied, would make enquiries in regard to the possibilities of obtaining accommodation elsewhere.'

Unfortunately, or otherwise, Cole was absent from this important meeting because of illness; nevertheless plans went ahead. A leaflet was printed for publicity purposes, in which it was stated 'Easton Lodge is remote from shops. Bring anything you expect to need'. There was also the promise that 'too much organisation will be avoided', but because there were 'excellent tennis courts and a good floor for dancing' students were advised to bring tennis racket and dancing shoes. The inclusive fee for the school was £2 a week. The final recruitment was 42 students, of whom 23 stayed for both weeks, and the six tutors included C. E. M. Joad, R. S. Lambert and D. A. Ross.

The daily programme was: 9.00–10.15, Seminars; 10.30–11.45, Lecture; 12.00–1.15, Seminars; and the rest of the day was free from formal classes.

The tradition of the tutors writing short reports on students started at this school. They gave brief but incisive pen portraits of what must have been an interesting gathering. To quote but one: 'Mr . . . is an old Marxian, but does not appear to know Marx, nor can he put up a good defence of his position. He has evidently done much expounding of his position to people who have not criticised it. He has apparently not thought much lately. Even if he were to do so, he dare not think freely. Still he is a keen arguer and keeps his temper.'

Cole's final judgement was that Easton Lodge was an 'ideal place for a summer school' that it had been a great success and was likely to have a 'lasting influence on the London movement'.

Before leaving Easton Lodge, another interesting episode is worth recalling. Such was Lady Warwick's generosity and her commitment to radical change that she envisaged her large, rambling establishment forming a study centre for socialism. With this end in mind, she approached the Labour Party to see whether they would enter into some kind of arrangement. When this was not forthcoming she turned to the Trades Union Congress, where the response was more positive. Discussions went on throughout the summer of 1925, and perhaps Cole was able to spare a few minutes from his duties as director of studies to make a contribution to the plans for what was gradually evolving as 'an international labour university'. Two existing establishments, Ruskin College and the London Labour College (then managed by the TUC), were seen as likely faculties of this novel institution. And who was intended as principal? No doubt Cole thought himself suitable.

The premature release of these proposals in the *Morning Post* caused something of a stir, but gloom on the protracted negotiations was cast by the gathering clouds of industrial strife, later to culminate in the General Strike. In spite of these dark days the General Council of the TUC still thought positively about the scheme, and proposed a levy of one penny a member to be spread over three years producing £50,000 to meet the costs of additions and alterations to the Lodge. This was a modest sum, to be raised in a painless way, it might be thought, but opposition was mounting against a scheme which was thought by influential unionists to mean residential education for a privileged minority. At the TUC's annual congress in August 1926, the final *coup de grâce* was inflicted. The doubtful honour for this achievement went to Jack Jones, MP, of the General and Municipal Workers Union (no relation of the Transport and General Workers Union's present General Secretary, who is himself a keen advocate of adult education). Opposing the levy, his oratory reached its climax when he asserted 'we have had experience of men who have gone to Ruskin College dressed as workmen who have come back dressed in plus fours, and immediately wanting to be general secretary of their Union. I do not object to going down to Easton Lodge or anywhere else – but only for a day. If I stopped a week I should get sick.'

Whether the scheme would have succeeded is open to doubt. Dame Margaret Cole wrote about this episode in her husband's biography and concluded that he would have spent the coming years half in struggling to keep the peace between warring factions, and half in begging for cash.

For Lady Warwick it must have been a hard blow, yet another example of the lack of gratitude she sometimes experienced. One wonders what she thought of the Joint Committee's absence of formal thanks for her hospitality – there is no mention in the minutes of any formal expression of appreciation, such as had been the case in 1914, when the provost and fellows of Eton College received a fulsome letter of thanks. At least, she was remembered by the students when they met at a reunion after the summer school at Toynbee Hall and passed a vote of thanks to be conveyed to the Joint Committee, the tutors, and to Lady Warwick and her staff.

They also made a special request that the school again be held at Easton Lodge in 1926. After some initial difficulties, Lady Warwick agreed to house the school, which took place between 17 and 31 July 1926. 'It is difficult' wrote the new director of studies, R. S. Lambert, 'to imagine grounds and premises better suited for a summer school than Easton Lodge.' The Joint Committee was also well satisfied with the arrangements and accepted the proposal that next year's school should again be held at the Lodge, this time for four weeks.

This was, however, not to be so, as Lady Warwick now decided to allocate her Lodge to one or two selected organisations, which unhappily did not include the Joint Committee. Accommodation therefore had to be sought elsewhere and Ballinger Grange, Great Missenden, was the next venue.

After a single stay at this establishment, further searches had to be made for alternative accommodation. Barbara Wootton refers in her autobiography to the difficulties of finding suitable premises 'but I usually managed to discover some stately-home-turned-boarding-school which was glad of a letting in the summer holidays.' As it happened the school was held on three occasions at Wycombe Court, Lane End, Bucks. The next address had more permanency – Stratton Park, Micheldever, Hants (seven schools, 1931–37), and finally, before the war (1938–39), there were two schools at Brickwall, Northiam, Sussex.

Just over a thousand students attended the fifteen tutorial class summer schools held during the period 1925–39. This was not a vast number but the teaching that went on at these schools, both formal and informal, must have had a far wider impact than the number would suggest. In her biography, *Growing up into Revolution,* Margaret Cole wrote about the 'Summer School that peculiarly Anglo-Saxon combination of holiday-making, sociability and more-or-less intellectual effort' (though earlier she asserted that the 'teaching nearest to "university standard" was given at university summer schools'). She also regretted that it was difficult to evaluate the influence of the summer school on the development of radical thought. Later on she asserted that 'in the 1945 general election a large number (over a hundred to my knowledge) of the Labour MPS had been trained as tutors or students in the adult education movement'. Not all, of course, had attended a London tutorial class summer school, but irrespective of whether they became MPS or not, a vast proportion must have acquired a solid training in citizenship which stood them in good stead during the troubled years 1939–45 and in the post-war period.

As well as the intellectual achievements, there were the occasional romances – the most memorable being that between Barbara Wootton and George Wright, a tutorial class member who had been an adult student at the London School of Economics. After meeting at the 1934 school at Stratton Park, they agreed to get married, which they did nearly a year later.

Another tutorial class institution, created well before the first world war and maintained throughout that period, and, with certain modifications till the present time, is the Saturday school. Perhaps the most successful of the inter-war period was that held in 1921, when the average attendance over the four successive Saturdays was 525. The students met at the following places: Bedford College, University College, King's College and the University of London main buildings at South Kensington. Each school commenced with a general lecture at 3.00 pm; the 1921 programme ran as follows:

H. J. Laski: 'The Foundations of the State'
Graham Wallas: 'The Psychology of Work and Thought'
John Drinkwater: 'Poetry and Life'
W. T. Layton: 'Economic Functions of the League of Nations'.

After tea, the students were divided into five different tutorial groups dealing with economics, history and political science, psychology, literature and art, and the history of science. Twenty tutors took part in this activity, all highly distinguished experts, who gave their services without charge. Of the total costs of the four events, £121 14s, the only item which related to lecturers' expenses was: 'Sir F. Bridge (choristers) £2 2s 0d'.

The last school to be arranged along these lines was in 1927, when there were three main speakers: Sir W. Arbuthnot on 'New Health', H. J. Laski on 'Conditions of Democratic Government', and Ernest Barker on 'Ancient Greece'. This might be regarded as a conventional programme, bearing in mind the recent General Strike, but Laski may well have enlarged on this event in his lecture.

Possibly because of the growing difficulties of persuading lecturers to give their services free of charge, the problems of organisation and the declining audience (260 in 1927), arragements were changed in the following year. The reunion took place at Bedford College one Saturday in May, with an enlarged audience of 325, whilst an autumn Saturday school, recruited from members of 'local working-class organisations', was held at Islington Public Library in September. Succeeding schools continued to demonstrate the skill of the organising staff in putting on some lively and memorable events. The Saturday school and reunion held at LSE on 24 May 1930 is one such example. The first lecture was given by J. B. S. Haldane on 'Breathing in Relation to Industry (The subjects dealt with will include the work of miners, sewermen, divers and airmen)' and the second by Lascelles Abercrombie on 'Can literature be taught?'.

FURTHER ADMINISTRATIVE CHANGES

Before leaving the inter-war years, reference must be made to important administrative changes that resulted from another enquiry into the constitution of the University. The appointment by the Board of Education in 1924 of a committee of enquiry (under the chairmanship of Hilton Young, who succeeded Lord Ernle) was greeted with more enthusiasm than had been shown for the Haldane Commission in 1910. Although there was still a feeling in university circles that reform could best be achieved by amendments to the 1898 Act, there was a willingness to assist the enquiry.

Both the University Extension Board and the Joint Committee presented evidence, though what was given orally unhappily was not published. The UEB was represented by Dr C. W. Kimmins and the Rev J. Scott Lidgett, accompanied by the registrar, John Lea, and the Joint Committee by what was clearly a more powerful team, Dr Ernest Barker, Sir William Beveridge, Miss J. P. Madams, W. Lowth, together with its organising secretary, John Davidson.

The written evidence makes interesting reading and reflected the divisions that existed with the UEB. After a full and cogent statement of its work, the Joint Committee made several important proposals. There was a plea that its lengthy title should be abbreviated to the 'Joint Committee for Workers'

Education' (a similar request had earlier been made to the Haldane Commission). More important was the claim for direct access to the Senate supported by the view that 'it would interest the Senate more immediately and more deeply in the work of tutorial classes'. They further made the pointed observation that 'the University Extension Board, interested as it is in the examination of schools, no less than in the conduct of extension work, is a body of composite interests, unable to devote itself singly to the development of the extra-mural studies of the University'.

There was some further speculation about the membership of the Joint Committee with a preference for representatives from the main colleges of the University, and from LEAS, the WEA and the tutors. Finally, another point was made, which has often been expressed, that 'the Colleges of the University should be invited to offer, wherever possible teaching work, facilities for research and membership of their Common Rooms to established tutors for classes'. This was seen to have potential advantages for both sides; tutors would have something of a home in a college and the stimulus of contact with its work, whilst colleges would have attracted to them tutors with the advantage of the experience gained by teaching workers.

The UEB was less radical in its written evidence, asserting that existing arrangements gave 'in practice very great freedom' both to the views of the Joint Committee and of the UEB. Reference was made to the 'very fine traditions associated with the term University Extension, which they wished to retain in preference to "the somewhat repellent term Extra-Mural" which in any case is misleading' (so it was asserted) 'because of efforts being made to bring University Extension students within the Colleges'.

As they may have sensed some opposition to their retention of the inspection and examination of schools, the UEB took some pains to justify this part of their work. It was reported how this had started in 1875 as a result of pressure from Convocation, in spite of hostility from the Senate to any scheme that might have duplicated the long standing matriculation examination, first introduced in 1838. As a result, ten or so schools had been examined annually without any certificates being issued to successful candidates. Under Statute 39 of the University of London Act 1898, the newly appointed University Extension Board took over these duties from 1902. Five schools were initially involved, including University College School and North London Collegiate School (influenced perhaps by Dr Sophie Bryant, its headmistress and a member of UEB).

In the early days, papers set for the matriculation examination were taken, soon to be replaced by those set by the UEB's examiners in consultation with the teachers. As the years went by the system became highly complex, with junior school, school (matriculation standard) and senior school examinations. Things became simpler when the general school examination was first introduced in 1918, involving 158 schools and 2,844 candidates, rising to 317 schools and 11,134 candidates in 1924.

The administration of this activity must have placed great burdens on the staff and UEB members whose monthly agendas were usually full of reports, results and other matters relating to examinations. Yet it all seems to have been conducted efficiently and sometimes with unexpected concern for candidates. In 1919, for example, the Vice-Chancellor authorised the registrar to accept entries from a school in Middlesex five weeks after the closing date, as the headmaster 'had forgotten to forward the entries at the proper time owing to ill-health consequent upon influenza' (a touching reminder of the now forgotten post-war epidemic).

A few years later in 1927, a more contentious matter came up for discussion at a UEB meeting when its inspectors reported unfavourably upon an authority's school building. This led to a sharp response from the offended authority in which the inspectors were asked to restrict their comments to 'curriculum, organisation, teaching and educational work'. By return of post came the rejoinder that the Senate required UEB inspectors to be concerned with 'school buildings and fittings in respect of the general requirement of health and education', with the final, gentle observation, 'if better accommodation were available, it seemed that a higher standard of work would result'.

These episodes, to judge from an examination of the minutes, were few and far between. The great bulk of its work with schools went on smoothly to the evident satisfaction of its members and officers. They claimed in their statement to the committee that there was a useful relationship between the inspection and examination of schools and the provision of teaching facilities. Many school teachers, it was asserted, attended courses organised by UEB, whilst some head mistresses and masters sat on committees of local centres. Moreover, it was possible for 'an official of the University visiting a school . . . to keep an eye on the possibility of opening a new centre for lectures. There was yet another mutual advantage – that 'courses provide those pupils who do not proceed to a degree (and these form a large majority of those who take the School Examinations) with an opportunity of continuing their studies, and those who have recently left school prove excellent material for the lecturer'.

When the Hilton Young Committee's report eventually appeared in 1926 it contained a few sentences acknowledging the views expressed both by the Joint Committee and UEB. In the event these were put on one side when the recommendations were drawn up. The Joint Committee's plea for direct access to the Senate was set aside with a recommendation for the establishment of a University Extension and Tutorial Class Board 'a strong executive body representative of the teachers and colleges of the University, of appropriate organisations concerned with adult education and of other bodies actively interested in the promotion of university teaching'. Furthermore, the committee came down firmly in favour of a single Matriculation and Schools Examination Board. When this was eventually set up, a last minute plea for four places on the new board to be assigned to extension representatives was declined, the final and irrevocable termination of two decades of pioneering work in schools.

The new statutes came into force in 1928 with the creation of the University Extension and Tutorial Classes Council, and its two constituent committees. In its first annual report the UETCC hopefully asserted that the new administrative arrangements 'should tend to increase greatly the effectiveness of this important branch of the University's activities'.

Efforts were now concentrated on the provision of adult education based on tutorial classes and extension courses. The division of the work into two 'sides' was inevitable, perhaps even desirable at the time, and, mystifying as it must often have appeared to the outside world, was well understood by administrators. Nevertheless, A. Clow Ford,[1] first as Extension Registrar, and later as director, was well aware of the need for close co-operation, and often expressed his views in memoranda. For example, in 1944 he reflected on the origins of tutorial classes, and their separate existence. The great majority of tutorial class students were thought (a) to have left school about

---

[1]A. Clow Ford, OBE, (1883–1954), studied at University of Lausanne, and was interned in Germany at outbreak of the first world war, when he played an active part in organising the Ruhleben Camp School with its 5,000 internees; appointed secretary in the External Department 1919; External Registrar 1921; Extension and External Registrar, 1936–46; first Director of Extra-Mural Studies, 1946–48.

the age of 14, and (*b*) to be unable to afford the fees paid by extension students. 'Hence it was desirable to have a different academic approach to the subjects studied and no examinations.' His seemingly simple proposals were, nominal fees for everybody and 'the form of teaching to be determined solely on academic grounds'. Change is a slow process in a large organisation, but recently there has been greater disposition to talk more about the need for unity rather than to reflect on the dualism that is rooted in the past.

Intermission 1939-45

The first official awareness in university circles of the growing international tension that was to culminate in the second world war, was a statement by the Vice-Chancellor at the meeting of the University Extension and Tutorial Classes Council on 3 October 1938. In the event of war, he declared, the UETCC would have to take emergency measures but, at that moment, no action, in his view, appeared necessary. A fortnight or so later an Emergency Measures Committee was appointed, of which the UETCC's chairman (Sir Allen Mawer, Provost of University College) was a member, but indecision still prevailed. But by the spring of 1939, war seemed inevitable and at its meeting on 6 March the UETCC came to some tentative conclusions about their work during a period of national emergency. They concluded that courses would virtually come to an end in central London and only a modest programme could operate in the outer suburbs. Given the prevailing mood about the possible impact of total war, they were equally pessimistic about future prospects because of 'the need for all energies to be devoted to direct war purposes, the limitations upon transport and the general nervous tension'.

When war was declared in September 1939, the Senate House was taken over by the Ministry of Information, schools and colleges were dispersed to the relative calm of the provinces, and staff, academic and administrative, were soon swept into the war effort. A skeleton staff was still retained to maintain both the extension and external aspects of the university's work, and the registrar and his staff found new accommodation at Royal Holloway College, Englefield Green. Even the University Extension and Tutorial Classes Council went into a state of suspended animation, having its last pre-war meeting on 3 July 1939 and not gathering together again until 16 December 1942. Furthermore, that meeting was not without its difficulties – for the registrar had to report that 'in view of the lapse of time and the need for economy, the minutes of the last meeting were not presented to the members for confirmation'.

The Impact of Total War

The war made considerable inroads into the provision for extension courses, as the figures (which include postal courses for diplomas) below indicate.

The number of centres diminished from 62 in 1938–39 to 16 during the first
year of hostilities, a trend which was to continue; moreover, only two new
centres at Richmond and the Newman Association were established during
the war (in the session 1943–44).

Session	Total	Postal Courses	Session	Total	Postal Courses
1939–40	47	12	1942–43	29	7
1940–41	30	12	1943–44	39	4
1941–42	38	12	1944–45	37	4

After the abandonment of the Michaelmas programme in 1939, because of
the threat of 'aerial bombardment', courses were resumed early in 1940 with
the vast majority, contrary to expectations, taking place in central London.
Only two or three centres, notably the Bermondsey Settlement and West
Ham, kept things going in the suburbs, with a total close-down throughout
the rest of the extra-mural area. Efforts were made to promote courses of
'special topical interest' and to offer short series of lectures as 'a respite from
war thoughts'.

Under the first category was included a course on 'Air Raid Precautions' for
engineers and architects held at Imperial College in association with the
Ministry of Home Security. Lectures were given by the staff of the Ministry,
and there was a field day at Stewartby 'where the effects of explosives were
demonstrated by a series of tests'. Of a different genre, and presumably listed
under the second heading, was a series of three lectures delivered by Dr
Murdo Mackenzie to 34 students at West Ham on 'How to resist nervous
depression in wartime'. Were they any better equipped, one wonders, to
tackle the challenges of total war, by having attended three lectures on
'How to conquer anxiety in war-time'; 'How to keep mentally fit despite
war conditions'; and 'How anxiety affects national behaviour'?

One of the most popular lecturers at this time was the philosopher, C. E. M.
Joad. Such was his appeal (well before his Brains Trust fame) that he was
able to attract an audience of 250 at the City Literary Institute for his three
lectures on the 'Future of Civilisation'.

Whilst extension courses languished greatly during the war, tutorial classes
went from strength to strength as is indicated by the following table:

Session	No of Classes	No of Centres	Sessional Entries
1939–40	59	25	870
1940–41	31	21	420
1941–42	52	30	887
1942–43	66	31	1,169
1943–44	88	37	1,571
1944–45	95	44	1,671

Early in the war, Barbara Wootton who, since 1927, had been Director of Studies for Tutorial Classes left to take up a part-time appointment in the Royal Institute of International Affairs, whilst the two staff tutors left to work in the Ministries of Food and Labour. Happily, Barbara Wootton was able to resume her duties during session 1941–42. Also at this time, two appointments were made of organising tutors in areas where there were 'good prospects for considerable expansion' of tutorial classes. Werner Burmeister was assigned to Essex and Mrs C. M. Dyson to north-east Middlesex. This led to a great expansion of activity, with solid foundations being laid down at a number of centres.

A galaxy of talent conducted these classes, including Joan Chissell, Margaret Cole, Norbert Elias, H. J. Eysenck, Professor G. W. Keeton, O. R. McGregor, Karl Polanyi, Mary Stewart, Mrs A. Blanco White and Barbara Wootton. One class which surveyed the social services, under the tutorship of Barbara Wootton, eventually had its researches published in an issue of the *Sociological Review*. The most popular topics were literature, psychology and economics, although, surprisingly, courses on postwar reconstruction were less appealing, two were listed under this heading in 1942–43, three in 1943–44 and one in 1944–45.

Little emerges from the official reports of the devotion of students and lecturers during this period. Occasionally there is an oblique reference to war damage, for example, during the session 1940–41 when the Victoria and Albert Museum was not available for classes. Very rarely there is mention of a tragedy of war. On Canvey Island a class lost one of its members during an air raid, but the class re-formed again shortly afterwards, pledging themselves to their studies with added vigour. The section on tutorial classes in the annual report for 1944–45 contains the following sentence 'When the history during these years is written, tribute will surely be paid to the London students who after long hours at work attended classes, and to their tutors who made difficult journeys daring dark streets to reach the meeting place, for studies often interrupted and always threatened by enemy attack'.

The fifteenth tutorial summer school was held at Brickwall School, Northiam, Sussex, under the shadow of war in August 1939, and, nevertheless, 77 students attended. Thereafter, with the exception of 1944, the school continued to be held every year. In 1940 new premises were secured at Crofton Grange, Buntingford, Herts, which proved to be 'an exceptionally happy find'. This venue continued to attract a good recruitment, reaching the record number of 146 in 1942. There was great disappointment over the failure to secure alternative premises when Crofton Grange was not available in 1944, leading the UETCC to assert that 'it cannot be assumed that the finding of suitable accommodation will be easy, even when the war is over. The only complete solution of this recurrent problem would appear to be the ownership by the university of appropriate premises in the country'.

WARTIME DEVELOPMENTS

There was one group of students who might otherwise have been forgotten, but for the devoted work of the registrar, A. Clow Ford, and his assistant, Ronald Knowles. These were the British prisoners-of-war interned in 88 camps during the period of hostilities. In May 1942 the UETCC undertook responsibility for the censoring and despatch of examination material, not only for the University but also for other examining bodies. From May 1942 to March 1944 parcels of examination papers were despatched by airmail via Lisbon to the various POW camps. Later, in 1944, a new and quicker air route was established through Sweden and this continued to be used until the last despatch was sent on 7 April 1945. Altogether 136 different examining bodies were involved in the scheme, some having special requirements such as the Chartered Surveyors' Institute with its request for set squares specially made of cardboard. The remarkable total of 17,600 candidates were supplied with 6,091 examination papers – an operation which generated many expressions of gratitude and appreciation. A sentence in the annual report for 1944–45 paid tribute to this work: 'To many prisoner-of-war candidates, it has meant not only that they were saved from mental inertia, boredom – or even worse – but that they are now returning to civilian life better equipped vocationally than before, or in some cases even having developed entirely new interests and pursuits'.

To enable diploma students with at least one-year's study to their credit to continue their studies, a war-time scheme of postal courses was introduced shortly after the outbreak of hostilities. Some dozen or so tutors wrote correspondence courses and assisted students in their private studies. For example, two leading scholars in sociology, Hermann and Karl Mannheim, produced a course on 'Social Structure' for students taking the Diploma in Social Studies – other tutors included Cyril Burt, Norman Gash, S. H. Hooke, K. B. Smellie and C. A. Mace. As the years passed by, the demand for this type of correspondence study declined. Still, an important experiment had taken place (a few decades before the advent of the Open University) but, like so many other events of this time, little remains by way of record, except the impressive teaching notes of an outstanding team of scholars.

Once London had settled down to war-time conditions the demand for diploma courses, especially in social studies, gradually increased. Three courses for this award were organised especially for civil defence workers at the Chelsea Polytechnic whilst a devoted group of Red Cross workers pursued their studies at the Hammersmith branch of the British Red Cross Society. Another centre which, both then and after the war, achieved great popularity for its courses for the Diploma in Social Studies was (as it was then called) the Westminster LCC Commercial Institute. One of the courses held at that establishment during 1941–42 on the 'Social Services and Community Organisation' was given by three lecturers, later to achieve great fame in social work, Miss Eileen Younghusband, Miss S. Clement Brown and Miss E. M. Batten.

But, whilst a modest amount of activity was being organised on the home front, the needs of service personnel were soon to engage the interest and attention of the UETCC. Early in 1940, the Vice-Chancellor took the chair at a meeting attended by representatives from the Services and from educational authorities in the extra-mural area. From this gathering emerged the London Regional Committee for Education in HM Forces, under the chairmanship of Sir Allen Mawer (Provost of University College and chairman of the University Extension and Tutorial Classes Council) with the University Extension Registrar, A. Clow Ford, as its secretary. Unfortunately the records of its activities are limited to the UETCC's annual reports and minutes, and from these can be put together an account of work of major importance.

What happened can only be surmised by reference to bald statements and statistics – thousands of lectures were given each session, 1941–42, 5,368, 1942–43, 15,000, and rising in 1943–44 to 22,000 lectures. Who gave the lectures and where they took place is not revealed – though Shenley Military

Hospital was mentioned, where, at the beginning of the scheme, 'about six people visited the hospital twice weekly to give instruction in a variety of handicrafts and to give informal talks on current affairs and other topics of interest'. There is a similar dearth of information about the teachers, though the London Regional Committee reported in 1941–42 that it had discovered a number of qualified persons including 'many experts on current affairs and nationals from the Allies who can speak of the way of life of their people before Hitler's invasion and under the German occupation'. Other activities included a Directed Reading Service, and fortnightly bulletin 'On leave in London'.

The expertise of the staff was also put to good use by the provision of courses in the methods of adult education for discussion group leaders in the Services. Towards the end of the war, these courses were used as a selection procedure for potential students for the Post-War Emergency Training Scheme for Teachers.

The presence in and around London of members of the allied forces and their civilian counterparts represented a new and potentially valuable audience for educational pursuits. As a result of a request from the Polish Government for a series of lecture-visits for its educationalists and administrators, a varied programme was held during 1942–43 under the direction of the principal of the College of St Mark and St John, Chelsea.

Another scheme, of special concern to the registrar, was a series of short courses from March 1943 on the 'United Nations', 'as a free offering to their war effort'. It was Clow Ford's idea that short courses lasting four days should be given on the economic, political and cultural aspects of the allies in the order of their entry into the war. The first three countries thus surveyed were Czechoslovakia, Poland and France, with a concert being given by artists from the different countries at the end of each course. The experiment was judged a great success and was repeated in the two following sessions. The series in 1944 dealt with Norway, the Netherlands, Belgium, Greece and the USSR, but unfortunately the course on Yugoslavia had to be postponed 'for academic reasons', and that on India 'on account of flying bomb raids on London'. The course on the USSR was alone in not being introduced by a distinguished national – the inaugural address was given by Sir Stafford Cripps. There was also another slight difficulty – few of the lectures could be given by native speakers 'owing to the fact that there were very few Soviet citizens available in the country'.

During the first four weeks of August 1942 another pioneering activity took place at the request of the Canadian Army Educational Services. This was a non-residential summer school intended mainly for Canadian and American personnel, but members of other forces were invited. Lectures were given by persons 'whose thought was likely to help in determining the attitude of Great Britain towards post-war problems'. These 'wise men' included Lord Macmillan, Chairman of the University Court, Sir Henry Dale, President of the Royal Society, and Sir Fred Clarke, Director of the Institute of Education. Visits were made to conventional establishments including the Royal Academy of Arts, Royal Courts of Justice, and Kew Gardens. The school, attended by 238 students (175 Canadian), was judged to be a considerable success and was repeated again in 1943 with a slightly larger enrolment of 270 students.

The last enterprise in this series was far more narrow in its nature, being restricted to Canadian service personnel about to be repatriated. It was clearly intended to have a practical bias – 'to familiarise small groups of professional persons with the current thought and practice in this country in their own field'. Instead of discussing matters of high cultural and political moment five groups were organised to survey police courts at work, the practice of nursing, the practice of medicine in London, the film–an art and an industry, and export trade (with special reference to the British market for Canadian products).

Another war-time innovation was the United Nations University Centre. A provisional committee to launch this scheme was appointed in the autumn of 1942, and later met to discuss details at the British Academy. The chairman was A. M. Carr-Saunders, Director of the London School of Economics, and other members included R. W. Seton-Watson, Gilbert Murray, and W. K. Hancock. The general purpose of the centre was 'to encourage intellectual co-operation and promote the scientific knowledge which is the necessary foundation for the work of solving international problems, both of immediate and of long-term reconstruction'.

Support for the proposition was readily forthcoming from various allied circles – Dr Beneš, for example, wrote 'As a former Professor of Sociology, I naturally welcome any effort to promote understanding between university teachers of different nationalities. At the present epoch, especially, such association is of outstanding importance.'

The matter eventually came before the University Extension and Tutorial Classes Council and they gave the centre their blessing in May 1943, setting up a small committee to give advice (members: Professor M. Greenwood, chairman of the University Extension Committee, A. M. Carr-Saunders, Canon J. A. Douglas, Professor W. Rose and Professor Seton-Watson). After receiving Senate approval in June 1943, the centre began its work and took over the arrangements for the United Nations courses. It also arranged seminars on Civil Service administration in allied countries, and, during the last session before the end of the hostilities, provided opportunities for discussions on 'Problems of Labour Legislation' under the direction of Otto Kahn-Freund and on 'Public Corporations' under H. R. G. Greaves. Its last major activity was a course on the 'Post-war Treatment of Germany' attended initially by an audience of 120, mainly of service personnel. But, with the collapse of Germany, many members were drafted into the Control Commissions of the UK and USA and the final attendance was about fifty.

Anticipating that the changed circumstances of peace would materially affect the centre's activities, the UETCC asked its advisory committee to produce a report. This was available at the end of 1944, and doubt was expressed whether the centre should remain within the University. It was agreed to support the centre's activities for the time being, but next year its future was again discussed. As some duplication was thought to exist with the work of the London Institute of World Affairs there was a suggestion that the two organisations might amalgamate, but this was found not to be possible 'the Centre had sought mainly to project and interpret the separate United Nations and to undertake some comparative study of institutions', whilst the Institute 'had aimed primarily at the projection of international problems and action'.

To resolve the issue Professors H. H. Bellot and V. T. Harlow were asked to produce their own recommendations. In their report, they asserted that 'it is not a function of the Extension Department to organise meetings for the promotion of international goodwill, its business is with the spread of knowledge'. Their major recommendation was 'that a division of the Extension Department be established for the comparative study of British and foreign cultures and institutions – to take the form of schools and seminars conducted as far as possible by foreign nationals, "properly qualified",' with the final proviso that these activities were not to be made 'an instrument for furthering the purposes of the public relations of foreign governments'. These findings were accepted by the UETCC and the Senate agreed to the establishment of an International University Centre in 1946, to permit the continuation of the work in a modified form.

PREPARING FOR POST-WAR RECONSTRUCTION

In 1942, the University Extension and Tutorial Classes Council had two matters on its agenda for 16 December concerned with activities after the war. One was expansively headed 'Post-war Reconstruction', but its contents were limited to a mundane request from a Senate committee 'to examine the possibilities of a reduction in the number of Diplomas awarded by the University in the immediate post-war period.' Although the UETCC set up a sub-committee to consider the matter, there is no record that any diploma was recommended for elimination. On the contrary, two new awards were being discussed before the end of 1945, the Sister Tutor's Diploma and the Diploma in International Affairs. There was also a proposal received in April 1945 from the National Institute of Industrial Psychology for a Diploma in Occupational Psychology. On being referred to the boards of studies in Psychology and Sociology, their considered view was that time was not yet ripe for such an award.

The emergence of the Diploma in International Affairs is worth a brief mention. In August 1944, the London Institute of World Affairs proposed the introduction of such an award based on various grounds. There was a growing interest in the subject especially amongst the Services, and many enquiries had been received from different organisations, one of which was specially mentioned, the Conference on Missionary Societies. A small committee, chaired by Miss G. Jebb (Chairman of the UETCC and Principal of Bedford College) was appointed (members, Professor H. H. Bellot, A. M. Carr-Saunders, Professors G. W. Keeton and C. K. Webster), to produce a report. They recommended the creation of a Diploma in International Affairs and drafted a scheme of study, consisting of:

(1) The history of the development of international institutions since 1815, (2) International law, (3) International economic structure, and (4) a specific period or subject.

The scheme was sent to the boards of studies in History, Law and Economics for their concurrence. The first two approved the idea, but the board of studies in Economics was more caustic in its comments and felt 'it had better not express any opinion which might make it appear to be accepting any responsibility either for the principle or the existing draft syllabus of the suggested Diploma'. They were also dubious about teaching international economic structure to students with no previous knowledge of economics. The various criticisms were noted by the UETCC and a fair amount of quiet discussion must have gone on behind the scenes, for the scheme of study was eventually approved by the Senate in November 1945.

The other matter which the UETCC had on its agenda for 16 December 1942 was a memorandum by the registrar on the 'Future of Adult Education'. This was the first statement to be discussed at council level, of what might broadly be called the rationale of the department, and merits some attention.

After noting the modest proportions of the last pre-war session 'quantitively extremely small' (9,000 students attending extension lectures and 1,200 tutorial classes out of a total population estimated at twelve million), Clow Ford estimated that the number of students could 'certainly be doubled'.

He then postulated three motives for adult education – not the clearest of statements but indicative of contemporary thinking. There was (a) 'the desire to improve vocational status largely on economic grounds but also from altruistic motives'; (b) 'the amateur spirit – that is to say the desire to pursue an activity for its own sake'; and (c) 'the social activity motive, that is to say the desire to become more effective as individuals in influencing the continuous process of social adjustment'.

Next followed seven areas of need, a curious mixture of the obvious, and almost, it must be confessed, of the obscure.

(1) Physical Education – 'intelligent attention must be given to games and sports, including dancing, and to the aesthetic and spiritual satisfactions that are associated with a physically fit person and with skill in performance, – in other words a healthy body and a healthy mind'.
(2) Sex Education – 'the commercially biased pseudo-enlightment now available is one of the major causes of unhappiness not only in the body and soul of the individual but spreading hence to all his or her social activities'.
(3) Science Education – 'the number of scientific men who actively concern themselves with the social consequences of their work is quite negligible'.
(4) Religious Education – 'the greatest need of our times is a sense of religious conviction'.
(5) Political Education – 'indifference to the daily conduct of our national affairs is largely responsible for the "blood, sweat and tears" that are now our lot'.

(6) Aesthetic Education – 'if beauty is one of three fundamental satisfactions that life offers, [what were the other two?] it is surprising how rarely the word is heard in any class room in the land'.

(7) Technical Education – 'it is a large social-educational problem whether our community would be better served by technicians who were slightly less efficient and more alive to the social implications in which their work is set'.

After this set of personal affirmations there followed views, some in accord with contemporary thinking. Adult education, he regarded, as a 'permanent national necessity, to be given much greater consideration by the University than its lowly status as "a sort of appendage to the University and not an integral part".' There was also the position of extra-mural lecturers and tutors 'somewhat adrift from the main stream of University thought', the remedy being membership of their respective boards of studies.

It was decided that the document should be sent to all boards of studies for comment. In her covering note, the chairman stressed that the memorandum was to be regarded 'as expressing the opinions of an experienced officer of the University'. Boards were invited to comment upon four main propositions:

(1) to suggest how far their field of study was suitable for presentation to lay audiences with a view not to professional training but to the formation of an enlightened public opinion;
(2) to approve the principle that extra-mural work should be brought into closer relationship with the main work of the University;
(3) to assist the council on academic matters; and
(4) to suggest means of bringing extra-mural lecturers and tutors into closer association with internal teachers.

Replies were received from fourteen boards by the time the UETCC next met on 24 February 1944, though a further eleven may also have responded to judge from a pencilled note in the bound council minutes for the meeting at which the matter was discussed. All the published replies indicated a general assent to the main proposition that extra-mural work was a worthwhile activity of the University. There were, however, a few critical comments. The Board of Studies in Chemistry, for example, dissented from the registrar's views on technical education – 'that technical efficiency – the aim and teaching in technical colleges – had a dehumanising effect on society'. 'Not at all' affirmed the board 'efficiency and humanism are seldom antagonistic'. As regards close co-operation between the two sides of the University, the main obstacle, according to the Board of Studies in English, was 'the lack of suitable academic qualifications in some of the teachers engaged in extra-mural work'.

The net result of this activity was a report which was received by the Senate with no further action being recommended. More positive, and presumably offering some satisfaction to the registrar for his labour, was a resolution from the University Extension Committee to the UETCC that there should be a very substantial increase (possibly 100 per cent) in their expenditure in the period after the war.

CHANGES IN THE STAFF

For the time being the memorandum was put aside, indeed, some of the issues, especially those concerned with the relationship between extra-mural and internal teaching, continue to be matters of lively discussion. With the imminent ending of the war, however, there were more immediate problems of staffing. After 17 years' service as Director of Studies for Tutorial Classes, Barbara Wootton resigned to take up a readership in Social Studies at Bedford College from October 1944. Tributes were paid by the UETCC to her 'high academic attainments, her wide intellectual sympathies, her administrative skill and her keen interest in adult education'. The continued expansion of tutorial classes since her appointment in 1927, especially during the difficult war years, was largely due to her drive and enterprise.

In addition, the registrar and deputy registrar were due to retire within the foreseeable future, all of which made it important for the UETCC to consider its staffing policy. In her memorandum Miss G. Jebb stressed the need for the council's work to have a common academic policy, asserting that 'the sharp demarcation between the administration of the two sides of the work seems no longer justified on educational or other grounds'.

A sub-committee was appointed to review the staffing matters and, over the next year or so, important decisions were made that were to have a major impact on post-war developments. At its first meeting on 7 December 1944 the committee recommended that the two posts of extension and external registrar, amalgamated in February 1936, should be separated. They further urged that 'an officer of the status of Registrar' should be

appointed as soon as possible to head the department concerned with
extension and tutorial classes. At the same time they pressed for the appointment of a new director of studies for tutorial classes. In spite of the arguments for having two appointments – 'Head of Department' and 'a Director
for a part of the work' – Clow Ford clearly disapproved of the division of
academic and administrative responsibility. He questioned the ability of a
single director of studies to have effective oversight of the wide range of
subjects taught in tutorial classes. Moreover, he stressed the need for closer
contact with internal staff, especially with regard to academic advice, and
made a request for an allowance of £1,000 for payments to internal teachers
for their help.

Having made up his mind that he would accept the post in the extension
rather than in the external department[1], Clow Ford was clearly determined
that the extension department should be regarded as a college, as he put
it 'for it is primarily a teaching department and the head should be responsible
for both the academic and administrative sides of the work'. There was
also the suggestion that an academic board of five to seven teachers should
be created 'who should be paid a retaining fee and advise on most of the
work of both extension and tutorial classes that is at present covered by the
Director of Studies'.

What happened to these proposals is not recorded, though correspondence
survives in which Clow Ford regretted the forthcoming appointment of a
director of studies 'which will inevitably prolong and perhaps perpetuate
the cleavage which exists between the Tutorial class side and the work of
the Extension side, a cleavage which seems to me to be based on politico-
social grounds and quite out of place in a University community'. Miss
Jebb's reply was an attempt to mollify feelings, she agreed 'that the closer
co-ordination between Tutorial Class side of work and the Extension side
is much to be desired, but in aiming at this I feel much concerned to ensure
that we preserve the traditions of the movement to which they owe their
development'.

As was expected, Clow Ford was offered the choice of becoming registrar
either in the external or extension department and, somewhat to the sur-
prise of his colleagues, he chose the latter. But he was still concerned about
his prospective title asserting that ' "Head of Department of Extra-Mural

---

[1]The external department deals with London external degrees.

Studies" was a mean and characterless title quite unworthy of the post which, by reason of the quantity and quality and variety of the work, is the senior post of its kind in the whole country'.

All came out well in the end. Instead of a director of studies, the post of academic adviser to tutorial classes was created and it was held by Harold Shearman with great distinction from 1945 until his retirement in 1961. Clow Ford was appointed as Director of the Department of Extra-Mural Studies and the way was set for the exciting developments in the post-war world, sustained by more generous resources than had been the case after the first world war.

Three Decades of Progress

Whereas there had been much eloquent talk about adult education during the first world war, culminating in the 1919 report, and little else by way of government action, things were to be very different after the end of hostilities in 1945. The Education Act of the previous year had clearly stated the duties of local education authorities especially with regard to further (which included adult) education – how they were to secure the provision of adequate facilities and to cooperate with other providers. Against this background there was much discussion, both centrally and locally, about post-war developments in all fields of education, not least in adult education.

Mention has already been made of the memorandum written by the University Extension Registrar on the 'Future of Adult Education', and the varied reactions of boards of studies. Of greater significance was a paper written by Barbara Wootton in 1943, which was meant to complement the registrar's paper, and was more concerned 'with the trees than with the wood'. This was a modest view of what is an impressive piece of analysis of university adult education, based on fifteen years' experience, and is as relevant now. First of all she writes about standards and, whilst admitting the impact of war conditions, saw that 'in University education we should unremittingly insist on work which makes considerable demands upon the student – no subject can be mastered unless he reads, writes and thinks for himself'. Any attempt to reduce these demands, she continued, would 'debase our intellectual currency and imperil the standards of the future'.

Her views on the tutor's position are equally apt – she concluded that the hybrid appointment of a teacher who combined internal and extra-mural work had much to commend it, though she was aware of the difficulties that might be encountered.

Perhaps the practical alternative was for the extra-mural teacher to 'give courses within the gates – he has something to contribute to the under-graduate and graduate worlds; left completely to himself he may develop a Cinderella attitude'. She wrote a few words about students, and her paragraphs entitled 'after the class is over' will strike a sympathetic note thirty or more years later. There were students who went on from one class to

another – 'the fault, if fault there was, lay in the lack of appropriate opportunities for progressive study' – then came the comforting thought 'the
range of possible study is surely wide enough to last a lifetime at the rate of
one night a week'.

Discussion about class-room accommodation still continues, much of it
similar to Barbara Wootton's views. She welcomed the idea of an adult
education centre but was adamant that it should accommodate all kinds of
activity – 'it is much better that educational work should be housed under
the same roof as other interests and pursuits than that it should be segregated
in a Highbrow Edifice'. Having experienced difficulty in finding suitable
premises for summer school, she was also in favour of residential accommodation in the country, managed by the university, for a variety of activities.
Her proposals were well received in both the Tutorial Classes Committee
and the University Extension and Tutorial Classes Council and were to
form the basis of post-war policy.

In passing, mention may be made of an extraordinary meeting of the Senate
which was held on 5 April 1944, to receive accounts of 'post-war needs'
from different colleges and institutions of the University. The Extension
Registrar presented his plans for the future which were couched in very
modest terms. He envisaged that within two or three years after the end of
the war, the demand for both extension and tutorial classes would probably
double. Ever anxious about the financial implications, he speculated that
the eventual deficit would rise to £3,000 for extension courses and £5,500
for tutorial classes. A plea for premises in the country for summer schools,
weekend and other courses was made, also premises for a Centre for Extra-
Mural Education in London, preferably on the University site. As a kind
of afterthought, he referred to the United Nations University Centre then
costing about £500 a year; 'after the war it might be expected to develop
and to cost £750'. Such were the visions for the future!

In March 1945, the UETCC convened a conference of representatives from
LEAs, the WEA and the University to discuss future prospects in the London
area. Much of the discussion dealt with post-war developments – 'the
widespread interest in problems arising out of the war will stimulate the
desire for knowledge', it was stated. Reference was made to the lack of
suitable class accommodation, and one wonders how the LEA representatives
reacted to the view that they had the primary responsibility in this area.
They were also reminded that they should continue to give grants to the

universities 'in such a manner as to leave them free, in consultation with the authorities concerned, to develop the work in the different areas as suits the circumstances'. The final items on the conference agenda were about consultation and cooperation, and there was also some discussion about regional organisation. These topics were much in the air at the time, being the subject of another conference convened by the LCC in May 1946. In spite of these meetings there was little positive action, and sadly it must be reported that the Russell Committee's proposals (1973) for this kind of consultation are not being implemented with any great alacrity, though the Inner London Education Authority is setting up a regional consultative body.

THE BEGINNINGS OF EXPANSION

By the beginning of the first post-war session, 1945–46, the staff had been reduced to the academic adviser, secretary, assistant secretary, and two resident organising tutors to deal with the tutorial class programme, and virtually only one officer, the deputy extension registrar, for extension courses. In the event, 140 tutorial classes were held during the session, a considerable feat of organisation by a staff of such modest dimensions. Any further expansion would urgently need more appointments, a matter which was discussed early in 1946 by the Tutorial Classes Committee. The needs of the greater London area were stated in a well-documented statement to be the following: one administrative officer, three staff tutors and four resident organiser tutors to develop north-west, and south Middlesex, and west and east Surrey, with additional staff appointments should the programme continue to expand on the basis of one administrative officer and two staff tutors for every 50 additional classes.

To tackle the challenge of an expected increase in demand for extension courses, Cyril Thomas was appointed in July 1946 in succession to the Deputy Extension Registrar, A. T. Mitcheson. Proposals for further staff were modestly limited to two 'administrative organisers' to be responsible for courses north and south of the Thames – posts which were filled in 1947 by David Hopkinson and Edmund King.

The new Director, appointed in 1948, was Allan McPhee, who had held a similar post at Liverpool from 1938. He began his career in adult education as staff tutor at Sheffield, during the war years also acted as hon secretary of the Liverpool Regional Committee for Adult Education in HM Forces, and was a scholar of distinction; he was the author of a definitive work on the *Economic Revolution in British West Africa*. When he retired in 1960 the steady growth of the department, which was to reach its full momentum in the next decade, was well under way.

Werner Burmeister succeeded to the post of Director in September 1961. After working in an educational settlement in south Wales during the difficult years of unemployment and stress at home and abroad, he came to London in 1941 as resident organising tutor. Except for some years as adult education adviser to the British Embassy in Bonn, a period as leader writer on the *Manchester Guardian* (as it was then), and a short term of office as Director of the Extra-Mural Department in the University of Manchester, he has given his working life to the service of adult education in London. Few extra-mural directors can have had such wide experience.

One of the most important documents produced regularly over the last thirty years has been the quinquennial statement of policy – usually a judicious mixture of realism and optimism. The document for 1947–52 gave an interesting account of plans which were to achieve varying results. It began with a résumé of the disappointments experienced after the 1919 Adult Education Report, ascribed to 'severe financial retrenchment' and rather obscurely to 'the inability of the many parts of the movement to clarify their respective functions and to find a means of integration'. There were references to more hopeful omens, such as the financial arrangements under the new legislation which were bound to be more generous, and there was the foundation of two important pressure groups, the National Foundation for Adult Education (since 1949 the National Institute for Adult Education) and the Universities Council for Adult Education. By the last year of the quinquennium it was forecast that tutorial classes were likely to reach 500, and there would also be recovery on the extension side – 'at least 200 courses by 1951–52 and the possibility of substantially greater increases'. Other proposals were for an adult college and centre, and there was the prophetic observation that 'accommodation in Senate House is now hardly adequate, and a possible solution would be to move out'.

In the event the expansion in the immediate years after 1945 was remarkable, as the figures below indicate. Over this period, the number of diploma courses increased steadily from 41 in 1946–47 to 126 in 1951–52; on the other hand the optimistic expectations about tutorial classes were not to be achieved, though the continued growth of three-year classes was (and is) a matter of satisfaction.

	University Extension Courses		Tutorial Classes	
	Number of Courses	Students Enrolled	Number of Courses	Students Enrolled
1945–46	n.a.	n.a.	140	2,518
1946–47	78	3,205	156	3,002
1947–48	136	5,244	180	3,288
1948–49	244	7,650	187	3,175
1949–50	283	8,149	192	3,345
1950–51	291	7,884	205	3,518
1951–52	285	7,523	200	3,495

The other proposals for a centre and residential college had a difficult history. The quest for a centre seems never to have been pursued with any great fervour, and at the end of 1950 it was finally abandoned. The reasons stated are interesting: 'in and near the Senate House there is a range of accommodation for lectures, courses and conferences, and there is danger in the Department becoming isolated from the main stream of University life'. But the search for common room accommodation for the staff was not given up. On the other hand, the idea of an adult college was fixed in the collective mind of the UETCC, and it was not until the early 1950s that financial considerations compelled it to be abandoned. Before reviewing the work of the department since 1945, mention must be made of the changes in the statutes. As already mentioned, the University of London Act, 1926, laid the basis for the work of the University Extension and Tutorial Classes Council and its constituent committees. Early in the post-war period these came under review, and the then Principal, Harold Claughton, proposed that there would be a Council for Extra-Mural Studies with a more flexible membership.

The changes envisaged did not occur until the approval of the new statutes in November 1951, and session 1952–53 was the first during which the new Council for Extra-Mural Studies functioned. The most important innovations were the inclusion of appointed teachers on the Council (previously they had to be members of either the Academic Council, the Council for External Studies or the Collegiate Council), and of persons on the University Extension and Tutorial Classes Committees who were not members of the Council. The net result has been the greater participation, both on Council and on the committees, of persons with an active concern for university adult education.

The Programme and its Responses to New Challenges

The last three decades have been a period of accelerating discovery in virtually every area of human knowledge. To communicate some of this information to the public and to help its active and intelligent members towards an understanding of the implications is the right and proper function of an extra-mural department. This is no new idea – the London Society was devoted to the extension of university teaching, and by implication of learning, to the general public.

The main differences between the London Society and the Council are the magnitude of the task, complicated by the cumulative nature of discovery, and the increasingly difficult problems of communication. What follows is a brief account of the enterprise and the efforts made to forge links between the department and teaching and research institutions, whether in the university or elsewhere. From this partnership there emerges a range of educational enterprises of great diversity which no other agency is so admirably equipped to promote.

In the 1950s a new era had begun in the range and quantity of the biological and physical sciences. To organise work in these areas, the department was fortunate enough to have the services of Edmund King (now Professor of Comparative Education at King's College) and later Donald Vanstone. Between them they constructed a solid foundation of educational activities to which other colleagues have made their own contributions – whether by lecture courses, weekend and vacation schools, or field activities. Some boards of studies in the University were anxious to establish links with the department, and the fruits of this cooperation have been advanced courses in crystallography, embryology, physics and other disciplines. The most devoted members of these courses were, and still are, teachers anxious to keep abreast of the latest developments in their subject areas.

The appointment of Harry Frost as staff lecturer in the physical sciences (1960) was a recognition of the need for specialist direction. The Diploma in Science Studies is an original attempt to communicate an appreciation of science and to provide a basis for a critical appraisal of its significance in modern society and in modern thought. As such, it is as relevant to the needs of the graduate as to the person without an academic background, but the response in terms of class enrolment has been disappointing. The question might well be asked: where are the equivalent audiences of the hundreds of Victorian working men and others who attended Vivian B. Lewes' lectures? Some are now in conventional areas of higher and further education – universities, polytechnics, and technical colleges – but perhaps the decline in the popularity of the sciences at all levels of teaching affects extra-mural classes as well as under- and postgraduate recruitment.

Nevertheless, some lessons may be learned from the efforts of the early pioneers. One of the series of the People's Lectures in 1887 held at the Vestry Hall, St Pancras, included a lecture on 'The Water Supply of London'. Nearly ninety years later the topic reappears for the second time, when Harry Frost gave a successful course on 'Waterways and Water Resources'. Perhaps the gradual awareness of pressing matters of technological and environmental concern will again bring members of the public into the lecture room, which still remains the best forum for well-informed discussion. In the biological sciences significant changes have occurred over the last two decades. In the early 1950s, students of courses in biology and botany were still engaged in the dissection of fish and the section of plants, in ways not dissimilar from those in Dr Hill's classes at Morley College in 1927–30. Gradually changes have occurred in method and content with growing emphasis on the economic and environmental aspects of the life sciences, as they are now called. Since Richard Bailey's appointment in 1970, an increasing proportion of the work is now in ecology and conservation with the possibility of certificate and, later, diploma awards.

Archaeology is perhaps the one subject that owes its development to the influence of a single outstanding personality, the late Sir Mortimer Wheeler. Not only did his name become a household word in the television series, 'Animal, Vegetable or Mineral', but it was inevitably attached to the theme 'Digging up History' (the title of a lecture at the tutorial classes Saturday school, 1954). Sir Mortimer also contributed to various lecture series as an expert on Romano-British archaeology. One of the department's most successful exponents of archaeology, first as part-time then as full-time staff lecturer, was John Alexander. His first courses were given at Goldsmiths' College (1952 onwards), and he and other lecturers stimulated a growing demand for the subject in its various aspects, which proved almost insatiable. Thanks to the work of Douglas Maylor and the generous support of various internal teachers and other scholars, especially Professor W. F. Grimes, a Diploma in Archaeology was eventually launched later supplemented by a Certificate in Field Archaeology.

One of the earliest 'digs' was part of the programme of the extension summer school at Wye College (1952). A devoted and energetic team of amateur excavators spent some of their daily programme digging away under the broiling sunshine on the crest of Wye Down. Their finds were modest, but their pleasure was great when they received a visit and encouragement from Sir Mortimer Wheeler himself. More productive excavations took place in the city of Canterbury, and later work in the Cambridge area has been based on a happy partnership between the Cambridge and London extra-mural authorities. The diversity of archaeological pursuits continues – there has been a course in nautical archaeology at Seale-Hayne tutorial classes summer school, whilst other specialities include urban archaeology (with excavations directed by Harvey Sheldon at Southwark) and industrial archaeology.

International affairs unhappily remain low down the list of popular appeal, notwithstanding the efforts of both full and part-time staff. Nevertheless the London Institute of World Affairs played a notable part in the expansion of the Diploma in International Affairs. A roll-call of diploma holders who have since achieved eminence in their countries' affairs would present an impressive list of members of the staffs of embassies and commissions, including one former High Commissioner in London.

The ability of the department to respond to educational needs generated by legislation and new services is well illustrated by reference to courses in the social sciences. Of recent advances in social policy, one of the most significant has been legislation dealing with children deprived of a normal home life (including the Children Act 1948). This led to the creation of the Central Training Council in Child Care and its chairman, Sir Alan Moncrieff made approaches to the department in the late 1950s, in the expectation that arrangements might be made for a training course for child-care officers. This was not accepted at the time, but in its place a day-release course for workers without professional training was commenced in 1959 and held, appropriately enough, for the next few sessions on the premises of the Child Study Centre and at the Thomas Coram Foundation.

The Younghusband Report on Social Workers in Local Authority Health and Welfare Services (1959) and the important Local Authority Social Services Act (1970) led to considerable changes in the deployment of social workers, as well as growing pressures for more trained staff. In the meantime, a two-year part-time qualifying course for experienced social workers, of which Mrs Mary Pimm was the tutor in charge, had developed out of the day-release course. From 1968 until the last intake in the autumn of 1974, nearly 120 students were recruited, first from childrens' departments and related voluntary agencies, and then between 1970 and 1974 from the enlarged social services departments and other organisations, to be given a professional training.

The rationale of the course accorded well with the department's concept of adult education: it was run on a part-time basis, and was specially devised to meet the needs of students who had missed earlier opportunities for training. Although the word used is 'training', the approach by the tutorial staff (enlarged to include Miss Leslie Bell and Miss Ann Fontaine) was in the best traditions of liberal adult education. It also owed much to the distinctive teaching skills which such visiting lecturers as Dr Edna Oakeshott brought to the course.

Within two or three sessions after 1945 it was clear that there would be a rapid growth in demand for the Diploma in Social Studies, and this is borne out by figures in the footnote[1]. Meanwhile a diploma with the same title had been introduced for external students in 1948 and to avoid confusion some changes were imperative. For a few years, 1950–53, there was the Diploma in Social Theory and Social Structure, later replaced by the current Diploma in Sociology.

Student motivation in joining classes for this diploma, as well as deriving from a liberal interest in the subject, owes much to a vocational interest. This was further strenghtened by a scheme introduced in 1964 which enabled students in their third year of study for the Diploma in Sociology to apply for transfer to the External Diploma in Social Studies. The academic content of the course leading to the External Diploma in Social Studies was virtually the same as that for the Diploma in Sociology, but included, in addition, a period of supervised practical work. Various internal teachers envisaged the possibility of bringing the two awards together, and Miss Elisabeth Hunter, then tutor in social studies in the External Department, was of a like mind. With this measure of goodwill and support the transfer scheme was ultimately established, and an impressive group of holders of the Diploma in Sociology also achieved the External Diploma in Social Studies.

[1] 1946–47, 25 courses; 1947–48, 31 courses; 1948–49, 60 courses; 1950–51, 80 courses; 1955–56, 64 courses; 1965–66, 96 courses; and 1975–76, 60 courses.

Meanwhile changes were taking place in the wider framework of the External Department which entailed the running down of the system of external awards, save on the basis of private study. This meant that the Diploma in Social Studies was bound to have a finite life, notwithstanding the continued, indeed growing, demand from adult students, especially from women who had completed their child bearing and rearing experiences. With much regret on all sides the transfer scheme has come to an end, but such is the spirit of innovation in the department that another enterprise has been created with Mrs Joan Charlton as senior tutor. A new award, the Diploma in Social Work, was approved in 1975 by the University and the Central Council for Education and Training in Social Work. This has several distinctive features including the well-established tradition of part-time study and training.

The passing of the National Assistance Act in 1948 was hailed as a great step forward in social history: nevertheless, to adapt the service to the new post-war conditions was not possible without a major overhaul of staff recruitment and training. Once again the department was invited to play a small but significant rôle and from 1955, first the National Assistance Board (as it was then) and since 1974, the enlarged Department of Health and Social Security, have been its partners. During the first session of this relationship 17 courses on social policy and social development were arranged, and later the theme of the social services was added. Another pioneering venture was the series of seminars on 'Human Relations', first given by Professor E. Heimler (as he now is); a recognition by the board, and later by the Supplementary Benefits Commission, of the need to inculcate their staff in an understanding of claimants' attitudes and behaviour.

The courses arranged in association with the Church of England Temperance Society were some of the first in the field of criminology and were further developed during the years of partnership with the Institute for the Scientific Study and Treatment of Delinquency. A major advance occurred in 1963 when four extension courses on criminal law were arranged specially for members of police forces by Miss Monica Grobel, then Principal of the East London College of Commerce. They were held at Toynbee Hall and recruited a considerable body of students. There was clearly something of a pent-up demand for this subject and, to put it on a more substantial basis, the Certificate in Criminology was established in 1964.

Finally, in this field there has been a steady demand from the magistracy for opportunities to discuss matters of professional interest. As there are other agencies in the field the department has restricted itself to the educational needs of senior magistrates and since 1967, with the cooperation of the Lord Chancellor's Office and magistrates training committees, several highly successful courses have been organised.

As already noted, biblical and religious studies flourished in the thirties under the devoted guidance of Miss Marjory West. To commemorate her work and to further the literary and historical study of the Bible, the Frankland West weekend school was established on the basis of a generous gift by Miss Elsa West and a benefaction by Miss Marjory West. It was first held in 1964 and has been repeated annually with great success. Elsewhere the subject enjoys a sizeable response, especially to courses arranged in association with the Southwark Ordination Council, with a distinguished team of lecturers which lately has included Canon Fenton Morley (now Dean of Salisbury) and Bishop John Robinson (sometime Bishop of Woolwich and presently Dean of St John's, Cambridge). Other courses have been established with various denominational groups, including the Aquinas Centre, Institute of Christian Studies, and North London Zion House. The appointment of Michael Combermere as staff lecturer in biblical and religious studies in 1972 coincided with the growing interest in ecumenical matters. Courses in the world religions are now a commonplace feature of the department's courses, supplemented by some enterprising study tours to eastern countries – the latest being a visit to Istanbul in 1975 to study at first hand the Islamic faith.

Music has long been a popular subject, especially in tutorial classes, where Geoffrey Bush, senior staff tutor in music, has done much over the years to foster and maintain high standards of teaching and student response; he and other teachers have taught a small impressive group of students who hold the Diploma in the History of Music. Amongst his various enterprises Geoffrey Bush was responsible for the memorable concert (which included several items by composers who were also tutors) held at the Royal Festival Hall, in December 1963, to celebrate the jubilee of the London District of the WEA.

The latest development takes us back in some respects to the early days of the movement, when Canon Barnett and the residents of Toynbee Hall were endeavouring to create as he put it 'an oasis of sweetness and light' amongst the misery of the East End. Times and ideas have changed greatly but Stephen Parrott's appointment as staff lecturer in community studies in

1972 represents a concern for the continuing problems of social and educational deprivation. The area selected for his inquiries and teaching is the White City, and his work, which has wider implications for the department, has been actively supported by John Conway, Principal of the Addison Institute, and his colleagues. The Russell Report and its reference to community education and the disadvantaged stresses the urgency of this work.

Several certificates and diplomas have been introduced over the years and the various stages in their development may one day engage the attention of students of academic and organisational change. In the meantime, some brief comments may be made on three of these awards.

The Diploma in the History of Music was the outcome of various interest groups. From the first days of its establishment, the British Institute of Recorded Sound, then located at 38 Russell Square, was the venue of some notable lecture series organised by its secretary, Patrick Saul, in association with the department. The idea of a diploma which emerged from these activities was accepted by the University Extension Committee, and was evolved by an advisory committee under the chairmanship of Professor Bruce Pattison. Much expert advice was given by an outstanding musicologist and musician, the late Thurston Dart, and there was also considerable support from teachers within the department.

The genesis of the Certificate in Transport Studies was somewhat different. Transport education had been established at the London School of Economics from the 1890s and several generations of students, especially from the railways companies, had attended lectures in the evening. After the second world war, Gilbert Ponsonby (then Reader in Economics with special reference to transport) was anxious to transfer these courses, which in any case were beginning to decline, to another establishment. Having heard that the department was interested in this work, Sir Sydney Caine (then Director of the London School of Economics) accepted the idea of transfer and the first course in transport economics was arranged during the session 1954–55. Recruitment was enlarged to embrace students from all areas of the transport industry including the railways. Out of this growing demand a certificate (1959) and a diploma (1966) were eventually established, again on the basis of discussions, by an advisory committee under the chairmanship of Professor Michael Wise.

As a final example, the Certificate in Student Counselling may be briefly mentioned. Courses on the 'Management of Student Problems' owed their establishment to the labours of the late Dr Nicholas Malleson (then physician-in-charge of the Health Service for Central University Institutions and Director of the Unit for Research into Student Problems). He was much exercised about the economic and social costs of student breakdown and failure and was keen to offer those involved in student affairs – whether as chaplains, deans of studies, wardens of hostels or in any related capacity – an opportunity for organised discussion. The first course was held during the session 1963–64 and evoked a good response. Interest in the subject continued to develop, and it was clear that there was a need for a systematic course of study leading to an award. Happily the Master of Birkbeck College, Dr Ronald Tress, had maintained an interest in this area and agreed to become chairman of a small advisory committee to investigate the feasibility of a certificate. This was eventually established and the first intake of students was recruited for the session 1972–73 with Ellen Noonan as tutor/organiser.

Shortly after the end of the war, the Centre for the Study of International Relations was established, and it organised a small, but lively, programme of courses, supervised by a small committee under the chairmanship of Lord Hailey. It was eventually decided that this work should come under the purview of the University Extension Committee, and Allen Parker was appointed as administrative officer in 1947. He was succeeded as head of the Special Courses Section by Winifred Bamforth in 1955 when he left to become Director of the Department of Extra-Mural Studies, University of Birmingham.

Courses arranged by this section have covered a wide range of topics, and the section has done pioneer work in a variety of subjects, for example, courses for business economists, cooperating with such organisations as the Institute of Bankers, the US Educational Commission in the UK, as well as Schools of the University. A number of lecture-series have been published as symposia and a selection of them will give an idea of the range of the section's activities: *The Industrial Future of Great Britain* (1948); *Experimental Drama* (1963); and *Russian Literary Attitudes from Pushkin to Solzhenitsyn* (1976).

Another aspect of the work of the Special Courses Section also had its origins in the second world war. Immediately after the war there was acute need to make provision at British universities for American students at a time when British universities were themselves swamped with British applicants. Special provision was needed and plans were made to offer during the summer vacation, courses of a high academic standing and long enough for American students to obtain credit at their own university. The department assumed responsibility for organising the summer school offered by the University of London, and has continued to do so for thirty years. A six weeks' graduate summer school is held annually in central London. Students come from all over the world, although until 1976 about two-thirds of the total enrolment has come from the USA. The London School is offered in conjunction with similar courses held at Oxford, Edinburgh and Stratford-upon-Avon, and the universities concerned have acted together since 1953. The Department has been responsible since that date for the general coordination of the programme and the head of the Special Courses Section has also been secretary of the inter-university committee which sponsors the schools. London has perhaps been more adventurous than the other schools and has held courses in English law and in economics; but the subjects which command most interest are English literature and drama. London is, of course, strategically placed for presenting those subjects.

Continued Success of the Tutorial Class

The growth and development of the tutorial class provision, especially in the post-war years, merits a separate study to present the full story. As the figures below indicate it represents an outstanding achievement unparalleled

Session	No of Advanced Classes	No of Three-year Classes	Total of all Tutorial Classes	No of Enrolled Students
1938–39	4	62	66	1,156
1945–46	—	38	140	2,518
1950–51	6	115	205	3,518
1955–56	2	139	219	3,671
1960–61	6	136	226	3,952
1965–65	5	147	277	4,980
1970–71	7	186	350	6,780
1975–76	18	149	346	6,604

in any other extra-mural department. This solid edifice of work involving continuous and dedicated study, especially the advanced classes and three-year tutorials, has been created by several architects. The secure foundations were undoubtedly laid by Harold Shearman, who was academic adviser to tutorial classes from 1944 to 1961. At the time of his appointment he was educational officer to the WEA, having previously worked in the field as resident tutor, and to his office he brought the wider experience of a membership of a major educational authority, the LCC.

Fred Brook, who had been secretary for tutorial classes since the immediate post-war years, was appointed to the post of Deputy Director (Tutorial Classes), which incorporated the duties of academic adviser for that section of the work. He was a firm upholder of the tradition of systematic and independent study represented by the tutorial class. During his period of office, at a time when the will to make serious demands on students seemed to weaken elsewhere, the London programme grew vigorously. When he retired in 1972, his successor, T. F. Evans, inherited a body of work representing between a quarter and a third of the total provision of tutorial classes in the country.

But it is one thing to create a thriving administrative organisation at the centre – the work of organising classes has to be carried out at humbler levels and this largely means at the branch meetings of the WEA (responsible for over 80 per cent of the initial proposals for these classes). At these meetings resident staff tutors, now totalling nine, contribute their various skills as organisers, scholars and mentors.

Many classes take place during the day, thus affording opportunities for young mothers with family responsibilities and persons of retirement age to enjoy opportunities for liberal education and fellowship. Amongst the various events in the annual programme of the tutorial classes section the Saturday school and reunion and weekend school have long enjoyed considerable popularity. Two were particularly successful. The programme for the 1947 school (29 March) consisted of two outstanding lectures: Harold Laski on the 'Place of America in Modern Civilisation' (chairman, W. Lowth) and B. Ifor Evans (later Lord Evans) on 'Literature and Society' (chairman, J. Stewart Cook). A record audience of 1,068 gathered in the Great Hall of Friends House with extra places for tea having to be provided in neighbouring restaurants. Equally popular was the Saturday school which was part of the jubilee celebration of the original committee for tutorial class provision, the Joint Committee for the Promotion of the Higher Education of Working People (1909). A fortnight before the event 600 tickets were sold and a capacity audience heard a brilliant and provocative lecture by Barbara Wootton on the 'Reflections of a Sociologically-Minded Magistrate'. The chair was taken by Miss G. E. M. Jebb, Principal of Bedford College and chairman of the Tutorial Classes Committee from 1936 to 1951. In addition to the Saturday schools, there have been residential weekend schools at such attractive centres as Beatrice Webb House, near Dorking, and High Leigh, near Hoddesdon, Herts.

In the Russell Report on Adult Education (1973) there is a reference to the individual's need for 'rôle education', to enable him to discharge his duties more responsibly whether in society, in industry, in voluntary service or in public work of any kind. Various examples are given in the report of persons who might benefit from educational opportunities of this type – magistrates, policemen, social workers, shop stewards and trade unionists. The department has been increasingly mindful of these and other occupational groups, and has pioneered various courses for industrial workers.

The needs of this section of the community have been the concern of some of the most devoted adult teachers of the century – R. H. Tawney and G. D. H. Cole, for example. The Workers' Education Trade Union Committee (WETUC) was founded in 1919, to deal with adult education, but the number of enterprises organised by the University during the inter-war years was small. Since 1945 more time, effort and imagination have been devoted to this work. The first venture was a residential school on 'Trade Unions in Present Day Society' held at Beatrice Webb Memorial House in April 1949. The aim was to enable trade unionists 'to study problems which their movement will encounter in the light of its new responsibilities', and to give adult tutors opportunities for mutual discussion with trade unionists.

The appointment of Geoffrey Stuttard as staff tutor in industrial relations in 1959 led to increased activity in this field. Courses in liberal studies were arranged for apprentices at the Plessey Engineering Works, whilst the first day-release course for employees of the Glacier Metal Company at Wembley was held during 1961–62. Thereafter the work gathered momentum: in 1963–64 there were ten courses for industrial workers and in 1964–65 there were sixteen, of which fifteen were held in the firms' premises; of these no less than six were classes held at Fords in Dagenham. Day-release on a shift basis was started in 1966–67, and thirty students were selected out of a total of sixty applications from members of ASLEF, the engine drivers' union. The work continues at this modest level, but it is the policy of the department to expand its work in industrial studies wherever possible. The University of London, in common with some others, feels a special commitment to the great industrial community that it serves. Only the continuing difficulties of manpower and money, and the problems of the best ways in which to use resources, have so far prevented substantial progress.

WEEKEND COURSES AND SUMMER SCHOOLS

In the extension section residential weekend courses were developed by Douglas Maylor shortly after his appointment. Between March and June 1949 four residential weekend courses were held at the Battle of Britain House, Ruislip, Middlesex, and, at one time, the extension committee was responsible for nine courses a year at this centre. Elsewhere in the extra-mural area other centres have been made available; Haslemere Educational Museum, Wansfell Adult Education College, Debden House, Glyn House, Ewell, and Moor Park College, Farnham.

From early days of the extension movement, visits were sometimes arranged as part of the class programme, though not in any great number, and almost exclusively restricted to galleries and museums. Given the increased mobility of the population during the war, more often than not whilst on active service, it was not surprising that there was a growing appetite for class visits in the ensuing years of peace. Cheap party travel and chartered flights increased the feasibility of travel both within the country and abroad, and before long the era of the study tour began. It would appear to have been inaugurated with a visit planned and led by John Burrows to the Netherlands in May 1955. A group of sociology students were accommodated at 't Huis Kinhem in Bergen, where the warden, G. H. L. Schouten (later well known for his considerable services in building up the European Bureau for Adult Education), made them very welcome. The next enterprise, largely inspired by Sidney Hutchinson, holder of the Diploma in the History of Art, extension lecturer and secretary of the Royal Academy of Arts was a visit to Paris in 1959.

Thereafter increased interest was shown in this activity, and both students and lecturers became more enterprising, with parties travelling to Spain, Greece, Egypt and Nubia, Denmark, Sweden, Finland and the Soviet Union. Finally, there is the Anglo-German School, first organised in 1963. This was the outcome of Werner Burmeister's stay in Bonn, and the ninth school took place in 1976. The Anglo-German School has been held on a reciprocal basis in association with the Niedersächsische Landeszentrale für Politische Bildung (Centre for Education in Citizenship, Lower Saxony). Groups of eighteen students from extension and tutorial classes have spent

ten days in Hanover and Berlin. On their recent visit, the German partici-
pants stayed one week in London and another at one of the department's
residential summer schools. The very full programmes on both sides have
included formal lectures and study sessions on different aspects of contemporary British and German problems, visits to theatres, museums,
galleries and other places of cultural, political and social interest.

For hundreds of students who have attended the department's summer
schools, the week or fortnight spent in well-appointed premises in an
attractive countryside has been a happy and invigorating experience. Good
company, stimulating discussion and teaching, as well as a wealth of
recreational activities, are some of the ingredients that make these events an
outstanding feature of the department's annual programme.

Tutorial class summer schools have a long and unbroken sequence since
1922, with the exception of 1944 when it was impossible to find suitable
accommodation. Hearing about these difficulties shortly after the end of the
war, Mrs Mary Stocks (later Baroness Stocks), then a member of the
Tutorial Classes Committee and Principal of Westfield College, suggested
that one of her former students, Dr Violet Grubb, might help. Dr Grubb
was headmistress of Westonbirt, a leading boarding school for girls, and
she readily agreed to provide accommodation. Thus began an association
which has continued for thirty years. It is unlikely that any university
summer school elsewhere in the country can claim such a record of consistent success at the same centre. A considerable amount of time, energy and,
not the least, imagination go into the organisation of a summer school and
students at Westonbirt, Seale Hayne, and other centres, have been well
served with a variety of formal course activities, lectures, tutorials, visits,
field work and laboratory experience, as well as the equally important
informal social events. The twenty-fifth anniversary of the summer school
at Westonbirt, which was celebrated in 1972, also coincided with the
centenary of the building of the house, and a Westonbirt Anniversary Exhi-
bition was mounted by Mrs Peggy Mason and John Boulton Smith. This
comprised historical and architectural material showing the building of the
house and the laying out of the grounds and more recent exhibits telling the
story of the close association of the University with the school.

The culture of the summer school is a distinctive, if fleeting, phenomenon,
happily, it might be thought, unresearched by the social scientist. Yet the
pattern of relationships, the attitudes, behaviour, mores and so on of this

unique social institution is long overdue for the sensitive treatment by an imaginative writer – perhaps one of the tutors. In the meantime an agreeable footnote to the story of summer schools is a publication of 'a collection of the songs which form part of the revelry'.[1]

When Cyril Thomas organised the first extension summer school at Hillcroft College, in 1948, it was a small enterprise for students of economics and social studies with a warm and friendly atmosphere; later transferred to Crofton Grange, Buntingford, Hertfordshire, where the school was held for the next two years. Since 1951 the school has been held at Wye College,[2] the outcome of a happy partnership which began when Professor H. W. Miles and his colleagues gave courses on plant science shortly after the war in central London. Dunstan Skillbeck, principal until 1968 and his successor Dr G. Darling have continued to show a special interest in the school and some of the most notable courses have been given by the college staff, including Professor R. L. Wain. As at other schools, a wide range of courses in the sciences and the humanities is arranged, with social events and lectures by visiting speakers, two of whom – Richard Crossman and Enoch Powell – were both present at the 1955 school.

TRAINING THE TEACHERS

The main task of the department is the provision of courses of university standard. As the vast majority are taken by part-time staff, their selection and deployment are important matters of administration. This was recognised by the London Society in its early days, but the University Extension Board went further by providing a short training course in 1903. It was given by John Adams (Professor of Education in the University) and by Dr H. H. Hulbert, one of his staff at the London Day Training College. The syllabus consisted of the arrangement of lecture material and the management of the voice. Such was its success that the course was extended to three terms in 1908 and now included practice lectures by the students. Rather surprisingly, it continued to be offered throughout the first world war until 1918. Thereafter it became a series of terminal courses, often duplicated, on diction,

[1]*Songs from a Summer School* by Ronald Mason and Geoffrey Bush, obtainable from Peter Harris, University of London, Department of Extra-Mural Studies, 7 Ridgmount Street, London WC1E 7AD.
[2]Wye College, near Ashford, Kent, is the school of agriculture and horticulture of the University of London.

recitation and voice production until 1940, but, by now, the students were prospective actors rather than lecturers.

The relatively small number of lecturers and tutors taking part in the department's programme and the low level of turnover meant that much careful attention was paid to the appointment; applicants had to specify a time and place where they could be heard teaching. Moreover, classes were regularly visited, not only by the full-time staff, but in the days of the Joint Committee, by its members. With the impending expansion of class activities after 1945 it was evident that many more teachers would have to be recruited, and greater attention paid to their selection and training.

Towards the end of 1946, the Tutorial Classes Committee commenced discussions about training courses for tutors and were greatly helped by an important paper written by Harold Shearman. In his opening remarks, he referred to the report on the 'Tutor in Adult Education' published by the UK Carnegie Trustees in 1928. One of the quotations from the report is still relevant – 'While no amount of training for adult teaching will ever compensate for a lack of those qualities which are peculiarly essential to this work, carefully devised training courses can render valuable service in making easier the selection of tutors who possess the right gifts and sympathies'.

After noting the three main categories, the part-time tutors, full-time tutors (especially those commencing their career in adult education) and tutors appointed by the WEA for terminal and pioneer courses, he made two broad observations. There was first the possibility of treating adult education as the subject of a professional qualification, either a certificate or diploma. However, since the number of full-time appointments was likely to be small, Harold Shearman suggested a second approach, based on the needs of part-time tutors. His main recommendations were for short induction weekly courses (including visits to classes taken by experienced teachers), and for a similar course to be held at one of the committee's summer schools. He also posed the question: 'Is it possible for some lectures (and experience) in adult education to be included, as an optional subject, in the Diploma in Education course?'. The succeeding years have seen a growing provision of activities along these lines, with opportunities for prospective tutors to attend the annual tutorial classes summer schools.

On the extension side Cyril Thomas arranged the first two lecturers' conferences in 1947. Since then there have been many courses, conferences and seminars, concerned with teaching methods and subject content. Perhaps the most productive are those held at the beginning of the session for lecturers and tutors about to embark upon their first class. These are now regular features in the annual programme, as are conferences on the teaching of various subjects. Of the many enterprises of this latter variety mention must be made of the seminars for teachers of social history given by H. L. Beales, assisted by Professor O. R. McGregor. These began in the session 1952–53 and continued without interruption for nine successive sessions. Provision for adult education as an academic discipline arrived rather late in the day in the London area. It was not until 1971 that the Council for Extra-Mural Studies agreed to a proposal by the Director to establish a Diploma in Adult Education. An advisory committee was set up to work out the details, and amongst its members were some leading administrators and practitioners in the field, including H. L. Elvin, then Director of the University's Institute of Education and W. A. Devereux, then assistant education officer of the Inner London Education Authority. The collective wisdom and experience of the committee eventually produced a scheme based on two years' part-time study, primarily for those actively engaged in one or other of the various branches of adult education.

The senior staff lecturer appointed to supervise the new award was Elizabeth Monkhouse – a teacher with much experience in adult education, and equally as relevant, a member of the Russell Committee on Adult Education. The first intake of students was for the session 1972–73, and their success in achieving their diploma in 1974 was due, not only to their own efforts, but also to the commitment of the teaching staff, mainly part-time. Valuable help was given by R. Morris, Principal of the Stanhope Institute, in his contributions on the provisions of the local education authority.

STUDENT INVOLVEMENT

Because of their dispersion throughout the London area, students attending extension courses have often lacked cohesion and a corporate spirit. In spite of these difficulties there was a flourishing local centres' association in the early days of the movement, whilst the annual meetings of the London Society held in the Mansion House from 1886 to 1902 brought together hundreds of students.[1]

---

[1] A collection of the addresses at these meetings was published as *Aspects of Modern Study,* 1895, and included those given by Lord Playfair, G. J. Goschen, John Morley and Bishop Westcott.

In the early 1900s the University Extension Guild came into existence 'to foster and strengthen the University Extension movement', and membership was extended to 'all residents in London who are interested in General Higher Education'. To judge from the only source of information, the *University Extension Journal*, it was responsible for a number of interesting meetings, visits and lecture series, especially in Kensington. Two events may be cited to indicate contemporary interests. In 1911 a large audience at the University's main building in South Kensington heard a lecture by Sir Ernest Shackleton, with Fridtjof Nansen in the chair, on 'Nearest the South Pole', illustrated by slides and kinematograph pictures; and a year later, the students were presented with a demonstration of rhythmic gymnastics by Jacques Dalcroze and his pupils.

The University Extension Association dates back to 1921, but there are only brief references to its activities in the University Extension Board's annual reports and the *University Extension Bulletin*. In April 1948, a large gathering of extension lecturers and students meeting in the Beveridge Hall, at the Senate House, passed a resolution proposing the revival of the association and a provisional committee of sixteen was appointed. Professor G. W. Keeton, first president of the association, drafted a special constitution and rules and several hardworking and enterprising students and lecturers were ultimately recruited as the association's officers. Various enterprises were started, including the publication of a newsletter, the organisation of lectures, visits, socials and garden parties.

A separate Transport Studies Society affiliated to the central body was established in 1962 which over the years has built up a keen membership, and has organised an attractive programme of lectures and visits. The society has had a succession of presidents elected annually including Professor Michael Wise (the first holder of the office), Sir Colin Buchanan, Sir Peter Masefield, A. E. T. Griffiths, and Sir Daniel Pettit. Extra-mural students, many of them holding responsible positions in transport undertakings, arrange their own seminars to keep abreast of technical and economic developments of their field.

Over recent years, the University Extension Association has been dependent on a diminishing number of devoted officers, especially William Davies, chairman for several years until his retirement to north Wales, and Albert Eustance.

The student involvement in tutorial classes is of a more intimate and active nature. As a large proportion of the classes are arranged in cooperation with WEA branch committees, eighty in all, their membership, including active students, is a vital link with the WEA on the one hand and the University on the other. Some branches such as Harrow and Pinner and Croydon have had a long and continuous existence since the early days of the movement. The London District of the WEA is the parent body, so to speak, and has the rare distinction of being administered by two secretaries since its inauguration in 1913 – William Lowth and Stanley Church. A notable succession of officers have guided its fortunes at district and branch level, some, including Miss Rose Terry and Alfred George, having come to the WEA through the trade union movement.

Because of its close partnership of teacher and students the adult class tends to become a private world, though visitors, especially from the Extra-Mural Department, HM Inspectors, and those from local education authorities, are given, as it were, temporary membership. Occasionally classes have been inspired to produce work, whether articles or pamphlets for the general public, and these have invariably commanded much interest. The work of Mary Stewart's tutorial class at Ilford (1948) and an advanced class at Holborn (1958) is a good example of student activity producing some important findings in pamphlet form. These were two enquiries[1] into the leisure activities of school children at Ilford, and were based on questionnaires sent to 3,000 children in 1948 and to 7,000 in 1958. Other branches of the WEA have also produced valuable and original work under the guidance of their tutors, including local history classes at Pinner and Hatch End[2] (tutor, Elizabeth Cooper) and Farnham[3] (tutor, Anthony L. Crowe).

Effective publicity is a basic ingredient in the success of an organisation like the extra-mural department which carries on its activities over a wide area, and through a variety of agencies. Strong and active branches of the London District of the WEA have greatly assisted the development of tutorial classes, whilst local education authorities, through their institutes and centres, have proved effective partners in promoting extension courses. Publicity undertaken by the department, until 1951, was modest and

[1] *Leisure Activities of School Children in Ilford,* WEA, 1948 and 1958.
[2] *Harrow before your Time* and *Harrow Walkabout.*
[3] *The Cost of Living in 1300*; *Life Let us Cherish*: *A Survey of Poverty and Philanthropy in Farnham*; and *The Mild Prosperity of Farnham.*

amounted to a list of courses, printed in the format of official university documents. Later, when Werner Burmeister arrived, the department's literature was redesigned by Richard Eckersley and a new style booklet entitled *New Horizons* was produced.

With a body of something approaching 20,000 students, a vast amount of data has to be produced for various bodies, including the Department of Education and Science, local education authorities and the University. Since 1968, Robert Morris, in close association with the Management Systems Department of the University, has established new methods and procedures, based on the use of the computer, for basic information about students; it also enables the production of mailing lists.[1] In the same year a social survey was undertaken of a 10 per cent sample of the student population, selected by the computer. A brief report analysed the reasons why students joined classes, their reaction to the class and the class facilities.

The Extra-Mural Library began in a small way in 1910, when some 60 books were despatched to a small number of tutorial classes, at the request of the University Extension Board. These 'travelling libraries' as they were called were provided on a modest basis until the post-war expansion of classes. Miss Milne Clark, who entered the service of the University in 1938, was employed in this branch of the library from 1941 until her retirement in 1970, and built up what is now the largest library for the exclusive use of extra-mural students. The current stock consists of 170,000 volumes and 2,000 records. Every session 42,000 books are despatched to some 850 classes and six summer schools by a staff now consisting of six librarians.

VOCATIONAL AWARDS

As a result of its involvement in the inspection and examination of secondary schools, the University Extension Board was in touch with the aspirations of the teaching profession. It became increasingly aware of the demand for specialist qualifications not included in the initial training of teachers. From time to time other occupational groups expressed a similar interest in an award demonstrating professional competence. The UEB was well placed to look sympathetically at these requests, especially as statute 114 gave it authority to grant certificates of proficiency in any subject of study to any student of the University without the requirement of matriculation.

[1]For further details see Robert Morris, 'Computer-based administrative procedures in extra-mural work', *Adult Education,* March 1971.

The first of the vocational awards, as they have come to be known, was the Certificate in Religious Knowledge. It was established in 1908 to improve standards of scripture teaching in schools. The scheme of study was vague, with the exception of a directive that was issued to examiners. They were excluded from setting questions that might require the expression of a religious belief, and candidates were not to be penalised if they were likewise committed to a doctrinal view.

As might have been expected this vagueness, and the apparent belief that the certificate was mainly intended for school teachers and the weaker students in theological colleges, meant that there were very few candidates. The regulations were eventually revised towards the end of the first world war, with the requirements of the teaching profession and church workers being borne in mind. As a result, the certificate gradually achieved greater popularity especially after 1945.

Having pioneered the teaching of English as a foreign language at its annual vacation course (from 1904 onwards), the University Extension Board might have been well disposed to provide an award in this area, but it was not until 1920, at the suggestion of Daniel Jones, Reader (later Professor) in Phonetics at University College, that the Certificate of Proficiency in English was introduced. The special requirement of 'such acquaintance with Phonetics as may be of special value for teaching English in foreign countries' has generally been regarded as investing the award with considerable status. On the other hand this may have been responsible for keeping the number of candidates down to modest proportions, compared with other similar awards. The peak number of candidates was in 1935 when there were 235, since then numbers have declined.

Perhaps the most important awards have been within the field of nursing – a consequence of the State registration of nurses in 1919 (and earlier of midwives in 1902) with the inevitable quest for high professional awards. The first Diploma in Nursing was introduced in 1921 at Leeds, and this inspired Dr C. H. Bond, then a commissioner with the Board of Control, to suggest that the University of London might care to follow this example. The University Extension Board was gratified to learn that there were registered nurses who wished, by further studying and training, to fit themselves for posts of responsibility. As with other awards, a committee was set up to advise the UEB on establishing a diploma in this field, which was eventually introduced in 1926. Changes have since taken place in the regulations in accord with developments in nursing practice and theory, for example, in 1930 fever nursing was omitted from the curriculum. Another idea discussed at the time – that there should be three distinctive awards in clinical nursing, administration and teaching – remains a long-term objective.

The Salmon and Briggs Reports have led to important developments in the world of nursing. One of the results has been a considerable increase in the number of candidates for the diploma, from 144 in 1966 to just under 2,500 in 1976. A related award is the Sister-Tutor's Diploma introduced in 1945 and now enjoying considerable reputation and esteem. Discussions are taking place in the light of the Briggs Report, and a major change is likely to be the introduction of a Diploma in Nurse Education.

As with other awards, the creation of the Diploma in Dramatic Art resulted from a specific request – in this case early in 1922 from the governors, members and associates of the Central School of Speech Training and Dramatic Art. The University Extension Board eventually accepted the idea, and appointed an advisory committee composed of distinguished persons from the stage and the academic world including H. Granville Barker, Sybil Thorndike, Kenneth Barnes and Sir Israel Gollancz. Eminent persons in the theatrical world were asked to comment on the proposal and a reply, amongst others, was received from Bernard Shaw in which he wrote, rather curiously, that 'the differentia of the actor, which is acting, cannot be taught'. Undaunted by this negative statement, the committee went ahead and drew up a curriculum for the Diploma in Dramatic Art, with special reference to speech and movement, together with the appropriate literary and scientific studies. The first courses for the diploma were held in 1923 at the Central School and the Royal Academy of Dramatic Art, and for a short time at the Regent Street Polytechnic of Speech Training and Dramatic Art.

In 1949 the advisory committee conducted a systematic inquiry into the diploma, and concluded that it was a valuable background study for the craft of the actor and (with its third-year course) a basic foundation for the dramatic and speech training work of teachers and others. As a result of these discussions there were important changes in the syllabus which was again revised in 1963, with the now established principle that the diploma was suitable for all students intending to practise the dramatic and theatrical arts in any capacity, including acting. New circumstances and training possibilities have rendered the future of the Diploma in Dramatic Art uncertain.

The proposal for a Certificate of Proficiency in Natural History came initially from a technical college just before the war. Various education authorities were invited to comment on the idea, and much support was forthcoming. A committee was appointed to make recommendations, and a draft scheme of study submitted by F. H. C. Butler, inspector in biology for the LCC, provided a sound basis for the certificate, which was eventually established in 1939. As well as lectures and laboratory work, the course also involved practical work in the field. Inevitably the outbreak of war delayed the introduction of the certificate until 1942, when the first practical course was held at Royal Holloway College under the direction of F. H. C. Butler, still severely incapacitated as the result of injuries sustained in an air-raid. The next two courses were held at Cambridge, and in 1946 the venue was Flatford Mill. This was the pioneer field centre of the recently established Council for the Promotion of Field Studies, an organisation owing much to Butler's creative drive. Eventually recruitment was widened beyond the limited area of the teaching profession and another important innovation was the field test in both plant and animal ecology. This was introduced in 1956, and was thought to be the first of its kind in university examinations.

In 1966, the award was restyled the Certificate in Field Biology and the field work, already amounting to four weeks, now had to be undertaken at two centres. A diploma is envisaged, reflecting the growing interest in ecological matters and the management of the natural environment. The work is, finally, an excellent example of the cooperation that characterises the vocational awards; in this case, between the University, the Field Studies Council and its field centres.

When the full story of these awards is recorded, it will demonstrate the innovation and initiative characteristic of this aspect of the UEB's and later the department's work. Vocational diplomas and certificates have filled considerable gaps in professional training; they have materially advanced standards of competence and expertise, and, last but not least, they have been and continue to be available to students irrespective of their residence whether in London, the provinces, or abroad. Yet, when the time has come for other institutions to carry on the work, there has been no slavish resistance to change or adherence to tradition – these are the qualities of a mature pioneering body.

THE SUMMER SCHOOL OF ENGLISH

The origins of the Holiday Course for Foreigners (as it was originally styled) date back to the beginning of 1904, when the Senate received a request from a foreign government (thought to be German) for a vacation course of three to four weeks for foreign teachers of English. The proposal was accepted and a committee appointed by the University Extension Board to work out details. Although this was a new venture, earlier experience gained by the London Society in arranging two related enterprises – the University Extension Congress 1894, and the summer meeting 1898 – must have inspired a certain degree of confidence in accepting the challenge.

A powerful committee was appointed, which included Sir Edward Busk (Chairman of Convocation), Sir Arthur Rucker (first Principal of the re-organised University), Professor John Adams (Principal of the London Day College), Dr Charles Kimmins (by this time chief inspector of schools, LCC Education Committee), Dr Sophie Bryant (UEB's vice-chairman), Dr Frank Heath (at the Board of Education, and later joint secretary to the Haldane Commission) and two representatives from the Teachers' Guild.

Dr Walter Rippman (later Ripman) was the first director of the course, an office he held on 32 occasions until he retired in 1939. A total of 209 students (mainly teachers, 138 for the full course, the rest for the first or second fortnight) attended the first course which took place at the University's South Kensington buildings from 18 July to 12 August 1904. The course fee was £2 with students having to make their own arrangements for accommodation, assisted by a register of suitable private families, boarding houses and small hotels. The daily programme consisted of composition, conversation classes and lectures on various aspects of British life and institutions.

Having received the report that 'a spirit of friendly fellowship animated the students throughout the course', the Senate readily authorised the University Extension Board to continue with its arrangements for succeeding courses, until it was instructed to the contrary. As a result, the course (now school) has been held every year since its inception, except during the war years, 1914–18, and 1940–46.

Over the years, the venue and title of the course have been changed; the longest stay was at King's College of Household and Social Science, later Queen Elizabeth College (1934–66); since then it has been based at Goldsmiths' College. In 1936 it became the 'Holiday Course in English for Overseas Students', the result of a communication received from the British Library of Information in New York that 'foreigner' had 'an unfortunate connotation as a term of abuse'. After two more titles, it assumed in 1963 the present short and convenient 'Summer School of English'.

Distinguished university scholars have contributed greatly to the school's success, either as chairman of its advisory committee – Professor J. R. Firth (1948–56), Professor Geoffrey Bullough (1956–65), and since then Professor Bruce Pattison – or as its director. Recent holders of this latter office include Professor Pattison (1951–61), Professor Randolph Quirk (1962–66), J. D. O'Connor (1966–73), and currently Peter Hill. A secretary of the school was first appointed in 1938, and from then until his retirement in 1973, Ronald Knowles held that post with great distinction. To his devoted work over those long years the school largely owes its present, world-wide renown. His colleagues and friends, knowing something of this dedication, were greatly pleased when he received the honorary degree of MA from the University in 1974 as a token of appreciation of his long service.

The programme, both in terms of class tuition, visiting lecturers, and outside excursions, has become increasingly varied and comprehensive as the years have gone by. Many leading scholars, public figures and creative artists have enriched the school by their contributions – to name but a few, C. Day Lewis, Dame Edith Sitwell, Sir Michael Tippett, Victor Pasmore, Maxwell Fry, Richard Titmuss, Dame Ninette de Valois and Sir Pelham Warner (a notable expositor of one of our distinctive and, to foreigners, mysterious institutions, the game of cricket).

Although it has given rise to several imitators, the Summer School of English – the first of its kind in Britain – has the unassailable record of having recruited more than 14,000 students. In his inaugural address at the first course, Sir Arthur Rucker prophesied that it might become a great movement. Its fame across the world, and the achievement of its diamond jubilee in 1974, is an ample fulfilment of this forecast.

RETROSPECT AND PROSPECT

Two events have taken place in more recent times which focus attention on the department's achievements. In October 1959 the fiftieth anniversary of the Tutorial Classes Committee took place, and at the official reception there were several guests having links with the past, including Professor R. H. Tawney and a student in one of the first classes given by Henry Clay at Tottenham in 1909, Miss C. Westwood. Good wishes were received from T. S. Eliot with some interesting reminiscences of his classes at Southall, 1916–18, from Hugh Dalton, tutor in the 1920s, and Barbara Wootton, the former Director of Studies.

In his jubilee address, Professor Asa Briggs spoke of 'fifty years of concentrated and continuous effort, much of it undramatic, but the results of which have been of substantial social significance'. After stressing the virtues of tutorial classes which had set a standard for the whole adult education provision, he made a strong plea that 'the same qualities of leadership and common action that characterised the past fifty years be applied to the future'. If this were not to happen, he concluded, 'we may drift into even greater dangers than those which were expressed in the grim social abuses of the past'.

The second event, equally memorable, occurred in February 1968 when HM Queen Elizabeth the Queen Mother in her capacity as Chancellor of the University attended the reception of students who had gained certificates and diplomas during the session 1966–67. Accompanied by the chairman of the Council of Extra-Mural Studies, Sir Peter Noble, she spent an hour in lively discussion with some of the four hundred students present. This was recognition at the highest level of the achievements of adult students in gaining, largely by part-time study, a university award of widely recognised academic distinction.

The tutorial classes movement and the extension diploma scheme, both starting in 1909, represent the most outstanding feature of the last hundred years – the habit of innovation. The London Society, the University Extension Board and currently the Department of Extra-Mural Studies have continued to introduce new ideas of teaching methods and subject content, always reaching out for new student groups and adopting a more effective organisational framework. Seminars for social workers, day-release courses for trade unionists, courses for magistrates, transport managers, police officers and officers of the three Services, field courses in archaeology, geology and biology, and study-tours abroad, represent some of these pioneering enterprises. With the course leading to the Diploma in Adult Education, a start has been made with advancing the study of adult learning as an academic discipline and plans are now being made for more research and enquiry into a field of study which has acquired vital importance with the growth of recurrent education.

The vitality of any organisation depends on its ability to anticipate new developments, and the Department of Extra-Mural Studies has always responded quickly to new challenges. The acceptance of permanent education as a social, cultural and economic necessity formed the background of the Russell Report. Its recommendations in 1973 were criticised for being undramatic. They were based on the realistic belief that, for the necessary transformation of adult education, finance was more important than fanfares. Modest though its proposals were for roughly doubling the very small public expenditure on adult education over a period from five to seven years, they would have meant real progress in a field of education which affects the outlook and attitudes of the most alert, intelligent and active of our people in all sections of society.

In the absence of Government action, so far, the universities have once again taken the initiative, just as they did a century ago. The Committee of Vice-Chancellors and Principals, in cooperation with the Universities Council for Adult Education, have worked out development proposals which will not only provide more support for the established forms of extra-mural work but should also help larger numbers of mature students to get into first and higher degree courses and to extend the availability of post-experience courses for the renewal of knowledge. In London this has meant that the University with all its schools and colleges has looked at its own provisions in a domestic discussion which has greatly stimulated interest in all aspects of adult education and has led, among other things, to the conclusion that the remit of the Department of Extra-Mural Studies should be extended.

There is to be a closer relationship between the Department of Extra-Mural Studies and the rest of the University. The Adult Education Report of 1919 wanted the extra-mural department to become the 'eyes and ears' of the University. The University of London's working group on the future rôle of the Department of Extra-Mural Studies has stated in its interim report that the department 'already possesses experience and special expertise in various forms of part-time adult education as a link between the "internal" activities of the University, and the life of the London region. It should seek the most fruitful ways of communicating between the University and its institutions and the people within this region'. In spite of the immediate period of financial stringency, through which all education will have to pass, there can be little doubt that the University's extra-mural work will once again move forward to make a further essential contribution to the maintenance and development of an educated and democratic society.

Index